Contents

Enhancing Research-Teaching Links in Higher Education

Edited by

Simon K. Haslett

and

Hefin Rowlands

Proceedings of the Newport NEXUS Conference 2010

**Centre for Excellence in Learning and Teaching
Special Publication No. 3**

Published by the University of Wales, Newport.

Published 2010 by the University of Wales, Newport
Lodge Road, Caerleon, South Wales, NP18 3QT, UK.

© 2010 University of Wales, Newport.

Typeset in Myriad Pro.

Copy Editor: Vaida Andrijauskaite

ISBN 978-1-899274-43-7

Enhancing Research-Teaching Links in Higher Education
Simon K. Haslett and Hefin Rowlands (eds)
Proceedings of the Newport NEXUS Conference
Centre for Excellence in Learning and Teaching
Special Publication, No. 3, 2010, pp. 5-6
ISBN 978-1-899274-43-7

University of Wales, Newport

Prifysgol Cymru, Casnewydd

Enhancing research-teaching links in Higher Education: an introduction.

Simon K. Haslett[1] and Hefin Rowlands[2]

[1]Centre for Excellence in Learning and Teaching (CELT), University of Wales, Newport, Lodge Road, Caerleon, South Wales, NP18 3QT, United Kingdom. Email: Simon.haslett@newport.ac.uk

[2]Research and Enterprise Department (RED), University of Wales, Newport, Allt-yr-yn Avenue, Newport, NP20 5DA, United Kingdom. Email: Hefin.rowlands@newport.ac.uk

The links between research and teaching in Higher Education is a topic that continues to be discussed from individual departments up to keynote platforms in international conferences. There are two principal ways in which research and teaching may be linked, either in the curriculum (research-teaching nexus) or in research-informed teaching (Haslett, 2009a); both are equally important.

The Newport NEXUS Conference in 2009 had as its theme *Linking Research and Teaching in Higher Education* (Haslett and Rowlands, 2009) and represented the first institution-wide debate on the topic, with over 60 papers and keynote presentations. The fruits of that debate are becoming more evident across the institution with, for example, the launch of a new undergraduate research journal in the Newport Business School, planning for an undergraduate research conference in 2011, and raised levels of staff scholarship of learning and teaching (SoLT) and pedagogic research (PedR).

Recently, since NEXUS 2009, a number of important events have occurred in this field. Firstly, the anticipated monograph from the Higher Education Academy (HEA) on *Developing Undergraduate Research and Inquiry* has been published (Healey and Jenkins, 2009), and it is worth acknowledging that both authors have given workshops at Newport, and that Mick Healey is taking up a Visiting Professorship within CELT at Newport from September 2010.

Secondly, HEA Wales funded a two-day conference at Gregynog Hall in September 2009, convened by Simon Haslett, and facilitated by Mick Healey and Alan Jenkins, which was attended by representatives from all Welsh Higher Education Institutions (HEIs). This event was part of the activity of the HEA Wales Research-Teaching Nexus Action Set, and the main action from the conference was for a collection of case studies from Wales to be published (Haslett, 2010). Each Welsh HEI has contributed, with six from Newport, and is due to be launched at the end of June at the HEA Annual Conference at the University of Hertfordshire and at a future event in Wales. The work of the Action Set continues with the next workshop taking place at Trinity St. David's, Carmarthen, in September 2010.

Now that links between research and teaching are being actively forged at Newport and beyond, NEXUS 2010 aims to look at how these links may be enhanced to further enrich the curriculum, improve learning and teaching, and enhance the student experience. Also, it is important to encourage academics from Welsh HEIs to engage further in SoLT and PedR, as, for example, they are under-represented at learning and teaching conferences (Haslett, 2009b).

NEXUS 2010 comprises six symposia with over 50 papers, workshops and posters being presented, with some papers appearing in full in this *Proceedings* volume, but others in abstract form only. The symposium topics are:

- Creative Assessment, Curriculum and Pedagogy
- Flexible Learning in Employability and Community Scenarios (FLECS)
- Postgraduate and Academic Development
- Student Diversity and Engagement
- Sustainability and Geoscience Research in Higher Education
- Technology Enhanced Learning (TEL)

In addition, the Conference is fortunate to have five distinguished keynote speakers:

- Professor Brenda Smith (Higher Education Academy, York): *Issues in Assessment*
- Professor Richard Noss (Teaching and Learning Research Programme, London): *Technology-enhanced Learning*
- Heather Symonds (University of the Arts London): *Orality in Higher Education Assessment*
- Sir Adrian Webb: *Employability and Work-based Learning*
- Professor Cynthia Weston (McGill University, Canada): *Rethinking teaching in Higher Education*

Of the papers published in this volume, there is at least one from each of the symposia. Three papers are included here from the Creative Assessment, Curriculum and Pedagogy Symposium. Mark Jackson examines the level of creative ability of students born between 1980 and 1994, the so called 'Generation Y', whilst Elizabeth Nelson explores Foucault's concept of heterotropic space in relation to a new City Campus being built by the University of Wales, Newport. Sofia Nikolidaki looks at learning through a pedagogy using picture books.

From the FLECS Symposium, Alexandra Dobson and Jo Smedley discuss developing flexible learning in a 'Law for Managers' module using a blended learning approach. Two papers from the Postgraduate and Academic Development Symposium are also included; the first by Jo Maddern exploring the impact of coaching cultures on professional development and academic

identities and, the second, by John Spooner on developing an innovative practice-led methodology for a photographic PhD.

Alexandra Dobson and her Australian and Newport-based co-workers then, in the Student Diversity and Engagement Symposium, discuss the first phase of a project looking at the interesting use of biodata as a possible indicator of student withdrawal and retention.

From the Sustainability and Geoscience Research Symposium, a paper by Tatiana Diniz and Alison Glover reflects how practices on different scales, from local to global, contribute to effective sustainability, whilst Peter Brabham and Alessia Taboga present an interesting case study of how they link research and teaching in geohazards using local landslide examples from South Wales.

Finally, from the Technology-enhanced Learning Symposium, Julie Mathias and Tim Gillison look at interesting applications of technology on an 'Archives' course, whilst Joe Wan and his co-workers examine ways of engaging students in 3D virtual learning environments, such as Second Life.

NEXUS 2010 has all the ingredients of an exciting and vibrant conference that will contribute to the debate and enhance the body of knowledge in linking research and teaching in Higher Education.

REFERENCES

HASLETT, S. K. 2009a. Unpicking the links between research and teaching in Higher Education. *Newport CELT Journal*, 2, pp. 1-4.

HASLETT, S. K. 2009b. Higher Education conference attendance and engagement with the scholarship of teaching and learning: a Welsh perspective. *Journal of Applied Research in Higher Education*, 1 (2), 65-73.

HASLETT, S. K. (ed.) 2010. *Linking Research and Teaching in Wales*. York: Higher Education Academy.

HASLETT, S. K., ROWLANDS, H. (eds) 2009. *Linking Research and Teaching in Higher Education*. CELT Special Publication No. 1, University of Wales, Newport, 200pp.

HEALEY, M., JENKINS, A. 2009. *Developing Undergraduate Research and Inquiry*. York: Higher Education Academy, 152pp.

University of Wales, Newport	Prifysgol Cymru, Casnewydd

Enhancing Research-Teaching Links in Higher Education
Simon K. Haslett and Hefin Rowlands (eds)
Proceedings of the Newport NEXUS Conference
Centre for Excellence in Learning and Teaching
Special Publication, No. 3, 2010, pp. 7-11
ISBN 978-1-899274-43-7

The invisible average: an exploration of the perceptions of creativity within a group of 'Generation Y' students.

Mark Jackson

School of Art, Media & Design, University of Wales, Newport, Caerleon, Lodge Road, NP18 3QT, United Kingdom. Email: Mark.jackson@newport.ac.uk

Abstract

Over the past decade initiatives such as 'widening participation' (2003) and 'Gifted and Talented' (1999), have provided opportunities for higher education institutions to support the learning of defined groups of students who do not conform to traditional teaching methods. These policies have been particularly successful among students known as 'Generation Y' (born 1980-1994 and currently the largest demographic within Higher Education). The success of these politically sensitive initiatives however, only serves to highlight the plight of so-called average students within Design practice who show little progress in their achievement during their time in Higher Education. These students have a relatively successful school exam profile, are rarely identified as requiring any additional teaching support, maintain an excellent record of attendance, and engage significantly with all aspects of the curriculum. Academic staff often refer to this group of students as 'nice'. Using data collected from the UWN Design department over the past five years supported by interviews with current students, this study aimed to explore perceptions of teaching and learning and 'creativity' within this defined group of students. The goal was to determine the factors that should be considered if these students are to move from 'average', towards achieving their full potential.

Context

Of all the Education Reforms within the UK during recent years, the 'Future of Higher Education' Government Policy of 2003 has had the most tangible impact upon university course programmes, academic staff and students. Central to this policy was the recommendation of 'widening participation' within Higher Education by increasing student numbers, and creating and supporting opportunities for students from 'non traditional' backgrounds to benefit from the opportunities that education provides.

To support the learning needs of the increasingly diverse student body, Higher Education Institutions have been very successful at developing educational systems and programmes that support marginal groups, such as students for whom English is a second language (ESOL), or those who qualify for additional study support because of issues such as dyslexia or other learning needs.

Within this rapidly changing education landscape, perceptions of what constitutes the 'average' student have been increasingly challenged. Consequently the vast majority of pedagogic research over recent years has concentrated upon exploring initiatives that support this widening student base. Despite the success of the widening participation agenda however, higher education continues to be dominated by a generation of recent school leavers, commonly and currently known as 'Generation Y' (born 1980-1994).

As the lives of this demographic group have run parallel to the introduction and developments of digital technology within society, literature that investigates this group focuses primarily upon differentiating the attributes of this group from those of previous generations. Consequently we witness a wealth of research that examines this generation's relationship with digital technology (Prensky, 2001) or literature that explores the motivators, or transferable skills of this 'google generation' (McCrindle, 2006). As yet there has been very little interrogation of the impact of this technology upon 'creativity', or the 'creative' attributes of this generation of students, and yet there is a growing body of literature that identifies 'creativity' as an essential skill for the twenty first century (Robinson, 2001).

For the purposes of this study, the definition of 'creativity' follows the commonly accepted understanding of the term: as a process that produces an innovative or original outcome (Kleiman, 2008). Within the Art and Design community creativity is often subsequently aligned with innovation, with explorations of 'the new', 'the unknown', or challenging 'what we believe to know'. Implicit within this definition is therefore, an expectation or an embracing of 'risk'; without this 'risk', this 'leap of faith', design work is often destined to be predictable and repetitive.

Despite the wealth of 'learning outcomes' within undergraduate programmes, for academic staff within the Art & Design community, creativity remains the dominant attribute necessary as a determinant of success. So fundamentally, whilst students are being assessed on a range of skills, knowledge and understanding, they are inevitably being judged on their 'creativeness', with the highest achieving Design graduates often being described as 'creative' and 'innovative'.

Introduction

The Design Department at the University of Wales, Newport has been very successful over recent years at increasing student numbers by responding directly to the widening participation agenda and engaging these individuals with the benefits and opportunities afforded by working within a creative community. Creativity is central to the department's mission, and an implicit component of programme and project design and subsequent teaching methodologies. A recent analysis of student achievement data within the department, however, highlighted that whilst courses continued to produce very successful, 'highly creative' individuals, there was also evidence of a group of static 'average' students. These cohort members achieved the required learning outcomes, but demonstrated little progress during their studies in the quality and development of this 'success'. This group of students regularly complete their modules by deadline, and maintain a reasonable level of attendance, but consequently is rarely highlighted by exam boards or the Schools Quality Assurance system. As such they arguably blur into what could be termed 'the invisible average'. As a consequence, the aim of this study was to examine student perceptions of creativity within this group in order that mechanisms may be developed in the future which support their learning needs.

Using the results of exam board decisions over the past three years (2007/08/09) a sample group of 14 undergraduate Fashion Design and Graphic Design students were identified. This sample group contained individuals, who, in the duration of their studies, had consistently achieved a numerical average performance in their practical, or studio based work.

For the purposes of this study the 'average' grade was identified as C9 on the University of Wales alpha-numeric scale, equating to 55% on the more common numeric assessment system (in which 40% is identified as the lowest acceptable grade, and 70% identified as the highest grade boundary of 'First Class Honours'). Only studio based modules were accounted for, making the assumption that it was within these practical modules in which creativity and technical skills were being assessed, whilst theoretical components were used as a method of judging knowledge and understanding. The author acknowledges that many specialist staff for whom a more holistic approach to programme design is preferable, may have difficulty with this assumption, however, when one considers all module grades within a course programme there is rarely any consistency of grades at this 'average' level, and yet this is very evident when only the practice based module grades are considered.

Before interviewing the students, information regarding academic performance at both levels 2 and 3, was gathered from the Universities pre – enrolment system. This provided an overview of each student's academic history, whilst suggesting a correlation between this 'student type' and their future academic success. Each student was subsequently interviewed in order that they could elaborate upon their perceptions of this previous academic attainment, their domestic situation, their progress on their current programmes, and their perceptions of their creativity. These interviews revealed a number of common themes that challenge many of the assumptions held by teaching staff about the 'average' student.

Results

All the students within the group achieved a relatively successful academic profile at level 2 (GCSE), with every member of the group gaining at least 8 passes at grade C or above. Nine students had achieved at least one 'grade A', however these top grades were restricted to Art and Design in all but three cases.

At level 3, the academic performance was more varied, with students studying different combinations of qualifications. Whilst all the students had obviously achieved the necessary number of UCAS points necessary to gain entry to the undergraduate programme, only two students had achieved significantly higher grades than the required minimum.

During the interviews, all students within the sample group identified themselves as having very close supportive relationships with their family. Eight students still lived in the family home whilst studying, with another three individuals traveled home every weekend, sometimes traveling considerable distances in order to 'see family and friends'. The majority of the students discussed the 'security' and 'stability' of home, in addition to the 'comfort' of their surroundings. In 86% of cases, the parents were still married, whilst 57% students lived in detached houses with a minimum of four bedrooms.

Every member of the group had successfully applied for a student loan, and yet no students identified finance as being of concern, or affecting their studies. 65% of the group were employed in part-time jobs during term time, but in all these cases the students also owned a car, and cited part-time employment as a necessity in maintaining the vehicle (rather than the need to purchase course materials).

In addition to the economic information, students also discussed other factors that may impact on their decision-making, and influences on their creativity, and perception of the world.

Of this group, only one student identified having a parent with a higher education qualification, and yet several students cited 'parental advice' as being of prime importance in making their decision to study at the University.

More revealing still was their experience of travel. In previous generations 'travel' was often used as a discussion point at interviews for Higher Education. Experience of other cultures was seen as an important part of an individual's education. All of the students within the sample group had some experience of travel outside of the United Kingdom, however, this was mainly limited to the traditional holiday resorts of mainland Europe. Whilst 64% of the group claimed to have traveled more extensively this was specifically to Florida in the USA, and on holiday packages to Egypt. In all cases this travel was in the accompaniment of family and close friends. No students from the sample had traveled independently, or traveled to more unusual destinations.

Finally, students were asked to identify any other experiences or extra-curricula activities in which they participated which may be unusual, or affect their academic performance. What was most revealing about these answers was not the content or diversity, but the ordinariness of the results. No students were involved significantly in any sporting events, and rarely any activities outside of their studies and home-life. Two students described themselves simply as "quite normal".

As a conclusion to the interviews, each student was asked about their attitudes towards their current grade profile, and how they may improve them in the future. Whilst accepting of their marks, no student was satisfied with their grades. However, more pertinent was their responses to improved grades, which in all cases were mainly equated with 'increased effort' rather than talent, ideas, or the craft or style of their work, or indeed creativity. Instead their focus was entirely on the need for additional effort, which in some cases they were unwilling to commit to because of the assumed impact of other parts of their life.

Only one student cited the need to "step outside his comfort zone", yet also suggested "he was not prepared to take this risk". This evidence suggests that students within this group are not only relatively cautious individuals, but that they fail to recognise the implicit role of 'risk' within the creative process.

Risk Averse or Risk Aware?

In his work "Distinction – A Social Critique of the Judgement of Taste" (1984) the sociologist Pierre Bourdieu expanded his upon ideas of 'Cultural Capital' by exploring how the language and values of a social class are embedded within it's cultural currency. Subsequently, despite the rhetoric of a fluid and mobile social structure, access to a dominant social group is actually restrained by the 'Cultural Capital' of among others, a complex language of inference and suggestion. For Bourdieu therefore, the aesthetic 'habits' and 'tastes' of individuals are developed by exposure to these same 'tastes' and 'values' during childhood. Hence, despite the accumulation of wealth in later life, for many people their 'tastes' are already defined.

Whilst one can question this idea, the results of this study suggest that the 'low risk' culture instilled by parents during childhood as a 'safety net' are now actually preventing students such as this sample group to respond or indeed even be aware of the implicit need for 'risk' within creative subjects such as Design. This research suggests that these students are not necessarily 'risk averse', but are so conditioned by conformity, that they are not actually 'risk aware'.

Conclusions

Much of literature that explores the common attributes of this 'Generation Y' centres upon their confidence with digital technology (Prensky, 2001) along with many of the transferable skills that are frequently attributed to the multi-tasking necessary to fully engage with the converging Media landscape of the future. Whilst this literature is very positive about these young people, it fails to contextualise their upbringing within a wider social, political, and economic context.

Born between 1980 and 1994, this group of individuals has spent their formative years in one of the most politically stable periods within Western history. Whilst this generation has been exposed to a number of tumultuous international events, these have not directly affected these students. Instead their lives have run parallel to an extended period of political stability and relative economic affluence. While this may not provide the anarchy or hedonism exhibited by previous generations, it has arguably produced a group of very confident, well-rounded individuals who will clearly become assets to society in the future. For some individuals however, if this cultural stability is compounded by domestic security, this research suggests it may result in having developed a group of people who are perhaps conditioned and indeed contained by their conformity, and unless some intervention is made, are subsequently destined to remain the 'invisible average'.

Recommendations

Some of the most significant pedagogic research of recent years as developed from the exploration of an aligned curriculum suggested by Biggs and Tang (2007). This model links teaching methodologies directly with both 'aims' and 'learning outcomes'. Given our common acceptance therefore, within the Art and Design community, that 'risk' is an implicit component of 'creativity', it is interesting to note how rarely the concept of 'risk' is highlighted as a positive attribute within the main curriculum models of Art and Design, from level 2 through to undergraduate.

The conclusions of this study are speculative based on a small student sample. Further research is needed to more comprehensively explore some of the assumptions made. This initial investigation of 'average' Design students however, suggests that there is a need to highlight their secure domestic experience as a potential disadvantage within their academic progress, and to subsequently develop pedagogic models which develop 'risk taking' far more explicitly.

REFERENCES

BIGGS, J., TANG, C. 2007. *Teaching for Quality Learning at University*. Open University Press.

BOURDIEU, P. 1984. *Distinction - A Social Critique of the Judgement of Taste*. London: Routledge.

CUNLIFFE, L. 2008. Using assessment to nurture knowledge-rich creativity. *Innovations in Education and Teaching International* 45(3), pp. 309-317

GILL, T. 2007. *No Fear, Growing up in a risk averse society*. London. Calouste Gulbenkian Foundation.

HARGRAVES, J. 2008. Risk: the ethics of a creative curriculum. *Innovations in Education and Teaching International*, 45(3), pp. 227-234

JEFFRIES, K. 2007. Diagnosing the creativity of designers: individual feedback within mass higher education. *Design Studies*, 28(5), pp. 485-497

KENNEDY, G. 2009. *Educating the net generation – a handbook of finding for practice and policy*. University of Melbourne.

KLEIMAN, P. 2008. Towards transformation: conceptions of creativity in higher education. *Innovations in Education and Teaching International* 45(3), pp. 209-217

MASLOW, A. 1970. *Motivation and personality*. Longman

MACHIN, S., VIGNOLES, A. 2006. *Education Policy in the UK*. London, Centre for the Economics of Education.

McCRINDLE, M. 2006. *New generations at work: attracting, recruiting, retaining & training generation Y*. McCrindle Research http://www.mccrindle.com.au/wp_pdf/NewGenerationsAtWork.pdf [accessed 12th August 2009]

McWILLIAM, E. 2008. Unlearning how to teach. *Innovations in Education and Teaching International* 45(3), pp. 263-269

MOUNT, F. 2004. *Mind the Gap*. London, Short Books.

PRENSKY, M. 2001. Digital natives, digital immigrants. In *On the Horizon* 9(5), MCB University Press.

ROBINSON, K. 2001. *Out of our Minds – learning to be creative*. Capstone.

ROGERS, T. 2005. Measuring value added in higher education. *Quality Assurance in higher education* 13(2), pp. 95-106

WILLINGS, D. 1980. *The Creatively Gifted*. Cambridge, Woodhead-Faulkner Ltd

WILSON, M., GERBER, L. 2008. How Generational theory can improve teaching strategies for working with the millennials. *Currents in Teaching and Learning* 1(1) 2008, pp. 29-44

University of Wales, Newport

Prifysgol Cymru, Casnewydd

Enhancing Research-Teaching Links in Higher Education
Simon K. Haslett and Hefin Rowlands (eds)
Proceedings of the Newport NEXUS Conference
Centre for Excellence in Learning and Teaching
Special Publication, No. 3, 2010, pp. 12-19
ISBN 978-1-899274-43-7

An exploration of heterotopic space.

Elizabeth Nelson

School of Art, Media and Design, University of Wales, Newport, Lodge Road, Caerleon, NP18 3YG, UK. Email: elizabeth.nelson@newport.ac.uk

Abstract

The aim of the paper will be to explore the term Heterotopia, coined by Foucault in his 1967 work *Of other spaces (Des espaces autres),* that has remained a source of uncertainty and discussion ever since publication. Heterotopia, literally meaning 'other places', is a diverse concept that describes a world misaligned with respect to normal or everyday space. Foucault theorises heterotopias as places where the technologies and disciplines of social orders are out of sequence or momentarily suspended, then re-sequenced or reconstructed to generate new spaces where microcosms of society are transformed and cosseted.

Introduction

Heterotopia is a space where the public-private distinction is blurred. This could be a conceptual or physical borderline separating heterotopia from ordinary life, a contingent of systems, rules, practices and regulations that are distinct within heterotopia and that offer a sense of shelter or sanctuary. A particular kind of community develops articulated in inclusion/exclusion or insider/outsider distinctions. This paper will be an exploration into the term heterotopia and will attempt to contextualise the move to the City Campus by discussing new forms of public space situated within private space, for collective use. The transformation of Newport School of Art, Media & Design and Newport Business School within this new building will re-outline the contours of collective space bringing together a hybrid of public and private areas and an emergence of new working practices. This will interrupt the continuity and normalcy of our everyday space and intangible lines will be drawn and crossed to re-shape the space of the future.

Text

As cultural discourse deliberates the 'end of public space' (Sorkin 1992) and the demise of Hegel's (1820:1991) civil society we have cause to make use of an idiom, coined by Fredrick Jameson, the *postcivil society*. According to Jameson "this new special organisation is marked most dramatically by the disappearance of the public/private distinction" (1990, p.17). As the modern city is re-structured by contemporary architecture the outline of public and private space has become blurred offering new opportunities for productive environments but also allowing dystopian undercurrents to flow. This present-day cityscape offers the opportunity to re-visit Foucault's notion of heterotopia as a contemporary concept.

In a 1967 architectural lecture Foucault introduced the term heterotopia to describe an assortment of spaces, places and institutions where everyday society crossed the boundaries of normalcy in terms of their ordinary characteristics to interrupt stability; alterity enters the familiar. According to the author himself the term possesses often incompatible, multiple meanings which has led to it lacking one true definition. The discourse surrounding the lecture, that remained unpublished until 1984, has been one of encouragement and inspiration but also often of perplexity. Therefore, my aim here is not to define the term but to use its concepts, constructs and nuances to inform a reading of the new City Campus as a heterotopic space.

For Foucault the application of the term is bound up with the concept of time, where "the present epoch would perhaps rather be the epoch of space. We are in the epoch of simultaneity; we are in the epoch of juxtaposition, the epoch of the near and far, of the side by side, of the dispersed." (Foucault 1967, p.14) Long before Castells (1996) depiction of the network society and its space of flows, Foucault had developed his own entrenched pathway for life as a network of connecting dots and traversing points. The City Campus has been designed to become the juxtaposition between the different ideologies of the Arts and the Business schools (BDP 2007). Its aim is to bring the disparate together to produce new interdisciplinary and entrepreneurial working practices. Heterotopia is seen by some as being the preliminary construct for the *network society* (Dehaene 2008, p.14) and Castells depiction of space is indeed transparent in its relation to the purpose of the City Campus. Castells, like Foucault rejected the idea that space itself will disappear as we create a worldwide city because space acts as "the material support of time sharing social practices" the space of flows then becomes "the material organisation of time-sharing social practices that work through flows" (Castells 1996, p.147).

For Stickells, the network society has lead to the concept of a *heterotopia of flows* exploring the notion of "smooth spaces of urban mobility that generate new forms of public space" (2008, p248). The internal space of the City Campus has been conceptualised to enable various different forms of interaction with the building and to shape the circulation of different users through the

building, with a focus on mobility. Designed to flow both spatially and temporally with the public/private dimension also mobile, the formation of space will be predicated on activity, speed, traffic and flux rather than representing the more traditional forms of static occupation.

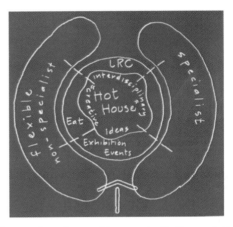

Figure 1. An architects draft *flow* of the building (BDP 2007, p.4)

By theorising the City Campus as a *heterotopia of flows* the building may invoke a space where the prospect of urban phenomenology (Bachelard 1992) could be realised; the excitement and pleasure of movement and flux. The two key phenomenological ideas of insideness and outsideness are immediately recognisable in the continuous arc of the roof that flows from interior to exterior. This is significant because it sets up an immediate relationship of synthesis between people, environment and space "creating a strong identity and promoting a sense of visual openness with the city context" (BDP 2007, p8). However, within this environment there is also the possibility of anxiety arising regarding the occupation of the space, with the physical and cultural location of users to be emergent through use. Spaces exploited purely for mobility and speed are often found to be lacking in terms of character and engagement. The concern here is that the multiplicity and changeability of spaces within the City Campus and the widening networks of public activity could lead to more demands for static space.

Emplacement is also an important suggestion within Foucault's text; how the space is defined in terms of its relationship and correlation between existing physical points and demographic points; "we are in an epoch in which space is given to us in the form of relations between emplacements" (Foucault 1967, p.15). The City Campus aims to create an "outward facing University Campus which visually and physically links with the wider city." Its architectural language offering physical transparency and inclusion, and its emplacement determined by and in support of the city's urban regeneration plans. It's aim of being at "the heart of the regions social, economical and cultural development" (newport.ac.uk) consciously mirrors a return for the arts school to the city centre. This hierarchical emplacement is also key in terms of widening access and engagement with the public, creative and business communities.

We often attach contradictory allegiances to space; public space and private space. We differentiate between "family space and social space, between cultural space and useful space, between the space of leisure and the space of work" (Foucault, 1967, p.16) these delineations can be conceptual or physical and are rarely the same from person to person. We learn from Bachelard's application of phenomenology to architecture in *The Poetic's of Space* (1992) of the psychological affects that the domestic space we live in, spaces loaded with qualia, have on our creativity. He defines how our imaginations are shaped and developed along the outline of the spaces we inhabit. He describes how by keeping us warm and safe shelters encourage the growth of our imaginations and how we recognise and appreciate the physical and metaphorical warmth of our homes when it's cold outside. This offers the conclusion that the space of our consciousness and the spaces of our primary existence are held together by qualities that seem intrinsic. Within the City Campus consideration for creativity and productivity must be given to whether the space we inhabit is a truly

transparent flowing space or an encumbered static space.

Figure 2. CGI image of City Campus

Figure 3. CGI image of Cit Campus in situ

Foucault defines heterotopia in terms of six principles. The first principle is that heterotopias exist in many varied forms across all cultures and that there is no universal truth. Here he defines the waning 'heterotopia of crisis': "...there are privileged, or sacred, or forbidden places, reserved for individuals who are, in relation to society and to the human environment in which they live, in a state of crisis" (Foucault 1967, p.18). He gives the example of privileged middle-class boys being sent 'elsewhere' (boarding school), set aside from society whilst they become men; a right of passage. He also refers to 'heterotopias of deviation' where people are displaced due to their behaviour being different from normal behaviour. He cites prisons, psychiatric hospitals and retirement homes, the latter being classed as a heterotopia of both crisis and deviation (he defines being elderly as a crisis and the prescribed idleness of age as a deviation).

The second principle determines that every heterotopia has a precise and determined temporal function within society. Within the text the temporal reference is heightened by Auge's (1995) reading of the delicate differences when translating French to English. For Auge, Foucault's discussion of 'space' is an abstract concept in relation to 'place'. Space can refer to a time period, or a locality, it's used by Foucault as an intangible term, whereas place has a sense of familiarity, of preconception. Here he uses the cemetery as an example; it has virtually always existed within western culture but in many different forms and in different physical places depending on the historical period of inspection. In the 18th Century the cemetery was situated at the centre of the city, in the church grounds. Drawing a parallel with bourgeois beliefs at the end of the 18th Century that the dead brought illness to the living, from the 19th Century, cemeteries were placed at the outskirts of cities. This displacement Foucault (1967, p.19) describes: "the cemeteries then no longer constitute the sacred and immortal belly of the city, but the 'other city', where each family possesses its dark dwelling." The City Campus can be defined as heterotopic in terms of the second principle because of its continued function through chronological changes and repositioning. This illustrates how the function of spaces change throughout their history to mirror the ideas of the time. Both geographical and ideological progress has been undertaken with the bringing together of Newport School of Art, Media and Design and Newport Business School to persuade entrepreneurial activities in the new civic heart of the city. In this case the geographical move is opposite to the one Foucault describes, as the building is moving out of the 'other city' back into the 'belly of the city'. In this instance the hope is that the effects of the new building spread virally due to the new geographic location. The space is meant to widen access and participation in terms of education but also to act as a restorative tool for a decaying city.

The third principles definition pivots on the partition of one space into several conflicting spaces or emplacements, producing surprising juxtapositions. Here the public/private divide can be brought back to the fore.

"The central aim of the design is to create a welcoming and inclusive building which caters for everyone. The intention is to encourage the widest spectrum of community engagement with opportunities for all to visit and enjoy the facilities in the new building" (newport.ac.uk).

Figure 4. Ground floor public entrance.

Upon arrival visitors (the public) will be able to access the "communal and shared space" of the exhibition area and café with views upward to the "heart space" of the building, as also will staff, students and affiliated parties of the University. Here the divide begins, this space has been designated public space by the very nature of its open accessibility and integration into the city, however students, staff and other members of the University may feel it a private space, themselves connected to the space by their hierarchical relationship with it. The effects of feelings of uncertainty on social cohesion could eventually lead to the distortion of that collective identity, allowing conceptual lines to be drawn that en-circle private space within public space.

As you move up through the building to the learning resources centre or library, by definition a very public space and developed as a serious of contradictory emplacements, you have a heterochronism[1] within a heterotopia. Although the general public do not have access, the University public do. It will be the most publically available space within the building, yet the necessity for private areas for quiet study and focussed research are also prioritised and you can see from Fig 6, the private spaces within the public space. Modern libraries can also be understood as extensions of the physical space they inhabit, their digital ecology intangible beyond the walls, they offer us controlling spatial codes that shape our understanding of their purpose.

Figure 5. Ground floor exhibition/café space

At the heart of the building the hothouse staff area will be inaccessible to the public yet will be a public space in terms of its open-plan design and shared accommodation. Intended to promote communication across the disciplines and a nurturing environment for academic creativity and knowledge transfer the space offers very little in terms of privacy. The space will become the product of the integration of NSAMD and NBS staff and the adaptation of a variety of institutional practices and operations. It would be interesting to track the cultural movements that take place within the first years of habitation, through the heterotopic reading of the space. Will knowledge transfer and interdisciplinary practise take place that wouldn't have done so prior to the City Campus?

By applying the third principle of heterotopia the City Campus and its various

real and intangible public and private spaces become heterotopic in their emplacement and in the way their elements are juxtaposed. Questions of which space sits comfortable next to which space and which space yields to make way for different interpretations will enable the mapping of social relations in terms of the spaces in-between, the break out spaces or Foucault's network "that connects points and intersects its own skein" (1967, p. 14).

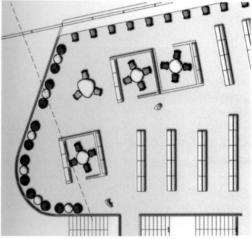

Figure 6. Detail from LRC plan

The fourth principle defines how heterotopias are temporally linked and are described by Foucault as "heterochronisms" (Foucault 1967, p.20) he characteristically describes heterochronisms as manifesting in two ways. Firstly it is envisioned that the space only starts to function as a heterotopia when the people who inhabit it are removed from their traditional time. The City Campus will propel the institution into a new time of shared cultural practises, pedagogies and space. Secondly, Foucault understands heterochronisms as "heterotopias where time accumulates indefinitely" the library or learning resources centre will become the very definition of this with its infinite accumulation of history and time. By accumulating all prior knowledge in one place, the library, becomes a place of everlasting and endless time, yet the space itself is outside of time and stationary.

---

[1] Foucault's term for heterotopias linked to "slices of time" (Foucault 1967, p. 20) discussed later in the paper.

Figure 7. Hothouse floor plan (BDP 2007, p.28).

The fifth principle of heterotopia is also temporal and presupposes a structured pattern of opening and closing that is dividing yet also accessible. For Foucault (1967, p21) "…one has to submit to rites and purifications. One can only enter with a certain permission and after having performed a certain number of gestures." Within the City Campus spaces will only be accessible to those with the permission to use them. Public access becomes a conciliatory expression as in principle the public will only have access to the ground floor foyer, cafe and exhibition space. If they want to head further inland they must submit to a series of security protocols. Students will be able to access the next level; the learning resources centre, the IT pods, the café, lecture theatres, studios and labs but will be restricted from entering the private space of the staff hothouse and above. Inflexibly their ID cards will only enable them access to their designated teaching spaces, diluting the interdisciplinary vision of the building. Depending on their role, staff will have the widest access enabling them entry to the hothouse, right up to the rooftop terrace. It's interesting to note that the "heart space" of the building, the hothouse, is the most private area in terms of admittance, accessibility fanning downwards and outwards.

The last principle of heterotopia is that it must function in relation to other spaces. For Foucault this sixth principle is based around illusion or illusory space. Here the heterotopic environment envisioned is a real space that leaves behind the original disorganised and unmanageable space to project forward a new showground, performing the same function as the old, yet that is painstaking thought-out and perfectly organised. This principle of Heterotopia makes palpable links with Baudrillard's text *Simulacra and Simulations* (1988). Here he that discusses reality, symbols or signs of reality and the incarceration of society by these factors. Baudrillard argues that contemporary society has substituted reality and meaning with signs or symbols of reality, and that humanity is now a simulation of this. The City Campus reflects the University as a combined and more perfect copy of its idealised self. This principle can be quite easily reconciled with the precise planning and forethought that has gone into the new building, discarding the peripheral in favour of a new heartland.

Conclusion

Heterotopia can be read as a construct by which to chart the various forms of communication between people, space and culture in modern society. The City Campus building is a heterotopia in its entirety, but there are also heterochronisms within the heterotopia, in particular the library, and can also be describe in its conceptual state a heterotopia of flows. Upon completion the City Campus should expressively demonstrate the essential relationship and required overlap between public and private space. However, this may change on it's occupation and actualisation.

Heterotopias often replicate and challenge. In terms of the City Campus this reproduction of two existing schools alongside the challenge offered by the shared space and proposed and premeditated expectation of interaction leads to questions of power. Not in the articulation but in the predicament of confrontation and contravention that follows. It could be said that Foucault's depiction of heterotopia mirrors his wider concerns with complex power relationships. The requirement becomes the avoidance of strengthening what your trying to breakdown. The City Campus's vision of interdisciplinary working practises and public/private spaces will be reliant on the equilibrium of power and heterotopia goes some way to offering an intangible spatial setting to overcome this problem of resistance. In a shared working environment (public) where interaction and the merging of boundaries between disciplines is the key philosophy, will paradoxically a growing number of people choose to work from home, a private space?

With regard to the buildings emplacement we are delivered into the physical proximity of the city and its binding elements. For a building based on free movement the city often offers an expression of diversity and collectivity. The layered effect of the public and private spaces offered within the same location may bring altercation. However, with that contact, conflict and communication comes the avoidance of isolation, the beginnings of plurality and "an additional space on which members of different, more limited publics talk across lines of cultural diversity" (Fraser 1992, p.126). Heterotopia can be a set of conventions inseparable from the dominant ideological arrangement but they can also augment and deflect from it. "We see heterotopia as being at the crossroads of the conceptual flight lines that shape public space today: the reinvention of the everyday: the ordinary and the extraordinary" (Dehaune (a) 2008, p.4).

In my view the City Campus will become a heterotopia, a space for collective educational, intellectual, public and economic use. The extent of the building, its internal arrangement and architectural design, will become signs of its power structure through culturally pre-determined societal relationships. Representation and reproduction of public and private space within one building will render the perception of convention obsolete. As a heterotopia the City Campus can be understood as a tool of analysis where dichotomies such as public and private space (and where the balance between the two is constantly changing) can no longer be sustained.

I'd like to conclude with a quote that reflects the positive possibilities of the City Campus and Bachelard's phenomenological thoughts on architecture; "With different degrees of relational intensity, heterotopias glitter and clash in their incongruous variety, illuminating a passage for our imagination" (Johnson, 2006, p. 87).

REFERENCES

AUGE, M. 1995. *Non-places: Introduction to an anthropology of supermodernity*. Trans John Howe. London: Verso.

BACHELARD, G. 1992. *The poetics of space*. Boston: Beacon Press.

BAUDRILLARD, J. 1988. Simulacra and Simulations. In POSTER, M. Ed. *Selected Writings*. USA: Stanford University Press.

BDP, 2007. *University of Wales, Newport: City Centre Campus, Phase 1, Architectural Stage D Report*. Doc No: P2001443/A/REP/003 Rev A

BLOOM, H. 1973. *The anxiety of Influence: A theory of poetry*. New York: Oxford University Press.

BOYER, C. The many mirrors of Foucault and their architectural reflections. In DEHAENE, M & De CAUTER, L. 2008. *Heterotopia and the City: Public space in a post civil society*. Oxon: Routledge, pp 53-75.

CASTELLS, M. 1996. *Rise of the network Society*, v.1. Oxford: Blackwell.

CENZATTI, M. Heterotopias of difference. In DEHAENE, M & De CAUTER, L. 2008. *Heterotopia and the City: Public space in a post civil society*. Oxon: Routledge, pp 75 – 87.

CRAMPTON, J. W. & ELDON, S. eds. 2007. *Space, Knowledge and Power; Foucault and Geography*. Hampshire, England: Ashgate Publishing House.

DEFLEM, M. 1991. Ritual Anti-Structure and Religion: A discussion of Victor Turners Processual Symbolic Analysis. *Journal for the Scientific Study of Religion*, 1991, 30 (1): 1-25.

DEHAENE, M & De CAUTER (a), L. Heterotopia in a postcivil society. In DEHAENE, M & De CAUTER, L. 2008. *Heterotopia and the City: Public space in a post civil society*. Oxon: Routledge, pp 3 - 9.

DEHAENE, M & De CAUTER (b), L. The space of play: towards a general theory of heterotopia. In DEHAENE, M & De CAUTER, L. 2008. *Heterotopia and the City: Public space in a post civil society*. Oxon: Routledge, pp 87 – 103.

FAUBION, D. J. Heterotopia: An Ecology. In DEHAENE, M & De CAUTER, L. 2008. *Heterotopia and the City: Public space in a post civil society*. Oxon: Routledge, pp 31-41.

FOUCAULT, M. 1967. Of Other Spaces. Trans, De Cauter, L. & Dehaene, M. In DEHAENE, M & De CAUTER, L. 2008. *Heterotopia and the City: Public space in a post civil society*. Oxon: Routledge, pp 13-31.

FOUCAULT, M. 1980. Space, Knowledge, Power. In FAUBION, J. D. ed. 2000. *Essential Works of Foucault 1954-1984, Volume 3: Power*. New York: New York press.

FOUCAUT, M. 2000. *Power: Volume 3*. New York: The New Press.

FRASER, N. 1992. Rethinking the public sphere. In CALHOUN, C. ed. *Habernas and the public sphere*. Cambrindge MA: The MIT press.

GOODMAN, P. & GOODMAN, P. 1947. *Communitas: Means of Livelihood and Ways of Everyday Life*. Chicago: Chicago University Press. (Available http://www.jstor.org/stable/2771317?origin= JSTOR-pdf)

HEGEL, G. W. F. 1991. Elements of the Philosophy of Right. ed, WOOD, A. W. Cambridge: Cambridge University Press.

HEYNEN, H. Heterotopia unfolded? In DEHAENE, M & De CAUTER, L. 2008. *Heterotopia and the City: Public space in a post civil society*. Oxon: Routledge, pp 311 – 315.

JAMESON, F. & SPEAKS, M. 1990. Envelopes and enclaves: the space of post civil society – an architectural conversation. *Assemblage*, 17: 32-7.

JOHNSON, P. 2006. Unravelling Foucault's 'different spaces'. *History of Human Sciences* 2006, 19: 75. (PDF supplied by author but can be found on line at http://hhs.sagepub.com/cgi/content/abstract /19/4/750)

McLEOD, M. 1996. Everyday and "Other" Spaces. In COLEMAN, E., DANZE, E & HENDERSON, C. eds. *Architecture and Feminism*. New York: Princeton Architectural press, pp. 1-37.

NEWPORT, UNIVERSITY OF WALES, 2010. *New Developments and the City Campus* [WWW]http://www3.newport.ac.uk/displayPa ge.aspx?object_id=8059&type=SEC (7 April 2010)

OCKMAN, J. 2001. *Book review of 'The poetics of Space'*. [www] http://www.gsd.harvard.edu/research/public ations/affiliated_publications/hdm/back_issu es/6books_ockman.pdf (31 March 2010)

PAWEL, Z. 2008. Tocqueville on Civillian Society: A romantic vision of the dichotomic structure of social reality. *Archiv fur Begriffsgeschichte*. Felix Meiner Verlag, 50.

SORKIN, M. ed. 1992. *Variations on a Theme Park, the new American City and the End of Public Space*. New York: Hill & Wang.

STICKELLS, L. The heterotopia of flows. In DEHAENE, M & De CAUTER, L. 2008. *Heterotopia and the City: Public space in a post civil society*. Oxon: Routledge, pp 248-257.

TURNER, V. 1969. *The Ritual Process: Structure and Anti-Structure*. Chicago, Illinois: Aldine.

University of Wales, Newport | Prifysgol Cymru, Casnewydd

Enhancing Research-Teaching Links in Higher Education
Simon K. Haslett and Hefin Rowlands (eds)
Proceedings of the Newport NEXUS Conference
Centre for Excellence in Learning and Teaching
Special Publication, No. 3, 2010, pp. 20-30
ISBN 978-1-899274-43-7

"I think therefore I participate": using a picture book in a philosophical inquiry with children and adults.

Sofia Nikolidaki

School of Education, University of Wales, Newport, Lodge Road, Caerleon, South Wales, NP18 3QT, United Kingdom. Email: sofia.nikolidaki@newport.ac.uk

Abstract

The aim of the workshop is to introduce philosophy for children (P4C) to a wider audience. Philosophy for children (P4C) was first introduced by Matthew Lipman in the 1970s as an attempt to apply philosophy in schools. Lipman, inspired mainly by Platonic dialogues, the Socratic method and Dewey's ideas on pragmatism, wrote a series of novels and accompanying manuals, so as to help teachers and children do philosophy in the classroom. The reason P4C was first introduced in the classroom was to develop children's thinking skills, particularly their ability to think critically, creatively and caringly. The workshop will begin with a brief explanation as to what P4C is and what do we mean by words or phrases such as 'stimuli' and 'community of inquiry'. Anecdotes from my personal experience from practising philosophy with children with a mixed group of adults and children in Newport will be also briefly presented. Then, attendants will have the opportunity to experience a P4C community of inquiry using a stimulus (in this case a picture book). The outcome of the workshop is to generate a philosophical debate and make the attendants realise that philosophising can be done not only through a formal academic process, but through dialoguing, exchanging and testing ideas as philosophy was first introduced in the Socratic tradition.

Introduction

Philosophy for Children (P4C) was presented and devised by Matthew Lipman in the early 1970s as a form of applied philosophy in educational settings. Lipman believed that philosophy was the appropriate tool to guide children's natural curiosity through the educational process, and develop children's higher order thinking putting emphasis on the parameters of critical, creative and caring thinking (Lipman, 2003). He introduced philosophical thinking to pupils aged 4-13, through a series of novels[1] (with accompanying manuals) whose main characters are children that present different models of philosophical thinking[2].

---

[1] Matthew Lipman was the first to write novels for doing P4C accompanied by their manuals. Harry Stotlemeier's Discovery was his first novel written for P4C addressed to 5-6 grade children and analyzing mainly Logic problems. Other novels followed such as 'Lisa' (concentrated mainly on ethics), 'Suki' (concentrated on aesthetics) and 'Mark' (focused on Social-political issues) for 7-10 grade children, 'Pixie', 'Kio and Gas', for 3-4 grade children and 'Elfie' for K-2 grade children. Ann Margaret Sharp wrote novels for younger children such as the 'The doll's hospital' and 'Geraldo' and their manuals which were co-authored with Laurence Splitter.

[2] Lipman, inspired by the pragmatist philosophers Charles Pierce and John Dewey, introduced the idea of a 'community of inquiry' as the natural environment where children convert from passive learners to active and collaborative researchers, who construct their knowledge and justify knowledge's truth by their mutual agreement,

The idea of doing philosophy for children has expanded, incorporating a variety of either different methods or styles of doing philosophy with children (PwC[3]), or the use of different stimuli such as picture books and works of art. Karin Murris (1992) introduced doing philosophy with existing stories[4] and more specifically picture books. She prefers picture books as they are usually short stories and children can focus not only on how the story ends, but also on other details within the story such as the illustration which can give totally different messages compared to the ones derived from the text (Murris, 1992, p.13). Furthermore, the young non readers can benefit from doing philosophy by listening to someone reading the story and getting the additional information from the pictures in the book (Scheinkman, 2004).

---

even if it is temporary. The teacher in such a community is not the holder of the knowledge and the one who provides information. S/he has the role of the facilitator who enables the philosophical dialogue by asking open-ended questions, asking for clarification and creating a supportive environment See for more information: Lipman et al. 1980. *Philosophy in the classroom* Philadelphia, PA: Temple University Press. Lipman, M. 1988. *Philosophy goes to School*. Philadelphia: Temple University Press and Splitter, J. & Sharp, A. 1995.*Teaching for better thinking*. Melbourne: ACER.
[3] For clarification's sake, when I refer to Philosophy for children (P4C) I refer to Lipman's approach of what is philosophy for children. Philosophy with children (PwC) is a broaden term that refers to all the other approach that involve doing philosophy with children, but Lipman's program.
[4] Tim Sprod (*"Book into ideas"*,1993), Sara Stanley (*"But Why?"*, 2004) and Robert Fisher ('*Stories for thinking- the Philosophy in Primary Schools (PIPS) project*', 1995) also encourage doing philosophy with stories which are more familiar to teachers and easier to get. Roger Sutcliffe's and Steve Williams's *"NEWSWISE: thinking through the news"* (2000) and *"THE PHILOSOPHY CLUB: an adventure in thinking"* (2002) offer support for using stories philosophically and are also linked to the English curriculum. Murris and Haynes' *"Storywise: Thinking Through Stories"* (2000) supports also teachers in using quality picture books and illustrations.

Picture books are distinguished from children's books, as the latter group are simply illustrated books. The illustration in children's books plays mainly a decorative role (Reeder, 1997). These books are not too rich for doing philosophy because there is no interaction between the two different systems: pictures and text. The word 'sophisticated' has been used for picture books to imply that there are refined connections between pictures and texts which could be interesting not only for children but also for adults (Burns, 1997b; Weller, J. 1984). The reading of the book on different levels is what can inspire both children and adults. In picture books philosophical wondering may start when the reader is puzzled by both images and text and activates his/her critical and creative thinking so as to derive meaning.

The method of doing philosophy with children has been expanded and has been used to doing philosophy with adults or mixed groups[5] (McCall, 2009). However, there is need for further empirical research on the impact philosophy has on both adults and children.

Aims of the paper

The aim of this paper is to work through ideas with reference to an example of doing philosophy with a mixed group of children and adults, using a particular picture book (Anthony Browne's *Zoo*). Particularly, the questions that this paper will address are:

- Can picture books activate children's and adults' thinking?
- Are there any similarities and differences between adults and children in the way they approach and cope with the same stimulus?

---

[5] I have tried PwC with mixed groups and also with adults (undergraduate students) at the University of Wales to deliver particular subjects from Ethics.

Methodology

The inquiry took place with a mixed group at a local library in South Wales. Fourteen members participated in this inquiry including the facilitator. The group was a mixture of adults and children of various ages[6] and was characterized for its diversity. It consisted of children and adults that were considered as people with low self esteem or low performance in school (for the children), who receive once a week for two hours extra support from adults who are willing to help them voluntarily. It was suggested to me to deliver some philosophical inquiries with both children and adults and see how the experiment would work. The findings described in this paper are from the second inquiry with the same group.

Framework for starting the inquiry

Children set the rules of teamwork before starting the inquiry. For instance, they agreed that they would: listen to each other carefully, not interrupt the others when speaking, not laugh at other people's ideas, agree and disagree with others providing, however, reasons. Then they shared a stimulus which in the particular inquiry was Anthony Browne's *Zoo*. Each member of the team read a sentence or a paragraph but had the right to pass in case the person did not feel comfortable reading. After the sharing of the stimulus the members had some time to think silently on their own and reflect on what they had just read. Then, they were invited to share their thoughts with the other members working in groups of three or four. The members of the groups changed their ideas and finally agreed to pose a question that would be interesting to investigate as a group or share it with others. When the teams were ready with the questions that they had posed, all the questions were announced and the

members found connections and links between the questions that other pupils had. The final list of the question was ready and the members voted for the one they would like to discuss to the greatest extent.

The selected question became the focus point for a discussion among children and adults that involve them thinking critically and creatively. The members of the inquiry tried to answer the posed question by arguing with each other and providing reasons for that, building on each other's ideas, clarifying their views, stating their ideas and wondering philosophically. The last member of the inquiry to speak would choose the next speaker. Usually one of the rules that was established in the first sessions was that people who have not spoken yet have a priority over the others and that the discussion should not be dominated by certain people. The facilitator intervened when the subject under discussion was obscure to some people and needed clarification, and when there were ideas that could be further or philosophically explored. Finally, the members of the inquiry summarized, reflected on the process itself and evaluated how well they thought they did.

Haynes (2002) mentions that philosophical inquiry is not a rigid step-by-step procedure but a process that depends on the quality of discussion and interaction. She also highlights the importance of listening to children's voices as a way of doing philosophy with them (Haynes, 2007). What is described above could be slightly differently delivered in another situation, with another group of people or even with another stimulus used.

The stimulus used

Anthony's Browne *Zoo* (1992) is a good example of a picture book that combines text with rich, detailed illustrations. While the text in *Zoo* describes a family's visit to the zoo, the illustration gives much more information concerning the attitudes of the family members towards the animals. This information wouldn't be aptly described verbally. For instance, some of the people

---

[6] The group consisted of : Helen (a), Hilary (child 6 yr), Judy (a), Joan (child 6 yr), Carmen (child, 11), Alina (a), Christina (a), Loukas (child 9), Paul (a), Jessica (a), Barbara (a), Chris (child, 12), and the facilitator (myself).

have animals' characteristics such as animals' feet, horns, beaks, animal print clothing and animals' expressions which are not always directly observable because one is so familiar with what one expects to see, that one doesn't see what is there[7].

Picture 1. The circles show humans with animal characteristics (Picture is taken from Browne, A © *Zoo*

Findings

The questions that the group come up with are displayed below. The first question was selected after a voting process in which people had two votes to distribute to different questions. The discussion focused mainly on the first question.

○ At the zoo, are the animals more dignified than the people? (Paul, Barbara, Chris) SELECTED.
○ Does the family respect the zoo and the animals? (Loukas, Christina and Janet)
○ Are humans the same as animals? (Alessandra, Joan, Carmen)
○ Is everything black and white? (Hilary, Helen (a) and Judy (a))

---

[7] This is an application of Gestalt theory, a psychological theory introduced by Max Wertheimer which refers to the function of the brain to organize given information and unify it to a meaningful whole, even if particular details do not necessarily lead to that whole.

Some moments of the discussion that occurred among children and adults are described and commented below:

1) *Children imaginative thinking and ability to observe details is sometimes better than the adults'.*

Picture 2 is taken from Browne, A © *Zoo*

a) There is a snail at the top of an image that depicts the traffic jam before the family goes to the zoo (picture 2).

Joan: Why is there a snail? Why does it fly?
Loukas: Maybe it is a spy?
Barbara (a): Or because there is too much traffic and even a snail goes faster?
Loukas: Yes, but why it is on the top of the page?
Hilary: If it was at the bottom we wouldn't see it.
Loukas: We would. It could be next to this pink car that has a pig tale!

In picture 3 there is the image of two giraffes in a cage. Their colour is the same with the colour of the wall making no contrast.

Joan: The giraffe licks the black paint because she does not have any food or water!
Facilitator: Why do you think so?
Joan: Because there is no black colour, she has licked it!

23

Picture 3 is taken from Browne, A © *Zoo*. The circle highlights what children's comments are about.

b) There is the image of a tiger in a cage (picture 4).

Loukas: Can you see the little butterfly at the bottom of the page? She has the same colours with the tiger. But the butterfly is free to fly. The tiger is in a cage.

Barbara: Did you see that there is only a little square on the top of the image from which the tiger can see a bit of the sky?

Loukas: And it is cloudy.

Paul (a): The sky looks as grey as the wall.

Loukas: Look at the grass. Outside it has a vivid colour, but in the cage it is pale.

Comments

In the first short dialogue, Joan feels free to ask two questions. Loukas and Barbara (adult) make hypotheses trying to answer Joan's question. Loukas asks a different question and Hilary makes a hypothesis to answer Loukas's question. Loukas is not satisfied with the answer about having the snail on the top of the page instead of the bottom, next to the car with the pig nail. There is a very logical structure followed in this example by adults and children for both to make themselves clear to the others.

Picture 4 is taken from Browne, A © *Zoo*. The circles bring into attention what children's comments are about.

Another interesting finding is the difference in imaginative and logical thinking among children and adults. In the first dialogue Barbara who is an adult and familiar with the metaphorical use of the language (snail=slow) offers a more 'logical' explanation of the possible association between the snail and the traffic jam by finding what they have in common, whilst Loukas has a more imaginative approach (a snail that is a spy). Even more of an unexpected and imaginative answer was offered by Joan in the second dialogue when she justified that the giraffes do not have plenty water. If the facilitator hadn't pushed her further to explain why she believes there is not enough water, Joan wouldn't make her thoughts clear. Her thought may look childish, but it is perfectly 'logic'. Joan associated the paint and the difference in colours (black and white) as it appears in picture 3. Joan linked these painting details together and associated them with the lack of water as a symptom of not treating the animals well.

This evidence agrees with the findings of developmental psychology that children have a more imaginative approach towards everyday issues (Matthews, 1994; Egan, 1988).

Children's experiences are often retrieved from the world of fantasy wherever it is found (e.g. in books, television programmes or videogames) (Egan, 1988). Pictures often enrich the story by narrating other aspects of it which can be in accordance with the text or contrary to it. It is one of the points where literature and philosophy meet. Murris (1992) referring to Egan considers picture books as an ideal place to present abstract binary concepts such as love and hate, beauty and ugliness and odd creatures, like witches and monsters[8].

Children can also think in metaphors[9] (for instance the snail as a spy) which shows a higher order thinking since they accomplish doing something really complex, such as linking a topic and a vehicle through a common ground. The topic is what the metaphor is about, the vehicle is the means by which the speaker refers to the topic and the ground is the sum of possible attributes shared by the topic and vehicle (Williams, 2002, p.17). The fact that children may have different ideas than adults, does not mean that they are illogical; children may have chosen different ways of linking a topic with different grounds which lead to an unusual metaphor. Adults listening carefully to children may realise the different ways children experience and understand their world (Haynes, 2007). Listening to the children is like opening a window and seeing world from a different perspective (Rorty, 1981). This can enrich our understanding of children and make us think what one's thinking gains as an adult but also what it loses (Egan, 1988).

Finally, it is fascinating to note children's abilities to pick up details and comment on them. Such an attitude justifies that children are more observant and driven by details,[10] while adults may have a more holistic approach about the understanding of a situation as can be explained through Gestalt psychology. When Loukas mentioned about the pig tail in the pink car, all the adults of the inquiry opened the books at the specific page to notice it and many admitted that they had not seen it before.

---

[8] Egan (1997) takes into consideration the imaginative aspect of children's thinking "the other half" of the children's thinking. Egan (2005) recognises three different stages from which children's cognitive development goes through: a) the mythic, b) the romantic and c) the theoretic stage. The first stage refers to the children aged 4-7 who understand the world in an imaginative – mythic way. The use of stories, metaphors, binary opposites, jokes, rhyme patterns, mystery and play are tools that match with the characteristics of children's understanding at this age and help them develop their understanding further. The second stage refers to the children aged 7-12 approximately. The mythic layer of how children understand themselves and the world is replaced by a romantic one. Children's cognitive characteristics that are displayed change so different tools can now serve their 'cognitive needs'. The use of heroes that gives the opportunity for children to identify with them, the sense of wonder, the need for reaching the limits of reality and experience, the narrative understanding (where things make sense in the context of a story) are some of the tools that can help children's cognitive development at this stage. See more: Egan, K. (1997) *The Educated Mind: How Cognitive Tools Shape our Understanding.* University of Chicago Press, Chicago. And Egan, K. (2005) *An Imaginative Approach to Teaching.* Jossey-Bass, San Francisco.

[9] Our conceptual system is highly metaphorical; the way we think and what we experience is, to a certain point, a matter of the metaphors we use in our language. For instance, conscious is portrayed often with the word up while unconscious is down

(up already/ fell asleep), more is up while less is down (e.g. my income rose last year/ the number of errors he made is incredibly low), good is up while bad is down (e.g. things look up/ things are at all time low) and so on. See: Lakoff, G. & Johnson, M. 1980. *Metaphors we live by,* Chicago and London: The University of Chicago press.

[10] Jean Piaget explains it as children concretism, which refers to children's inability to organize the information given by details in a meaningful whole. See more Piaget, J. 1929. *The Child's Conception of the World.* London: Routledge and Kegan Paul.

Even more impressive are Loukas's comments in the third dialogue. Loukas points to such a small detail (the butterfly at the bottom of the page), which is hardly noticeable, noting that it has the same colours with the tiger. He also points out that the grass has more vivid colours outside than inside the cage. Even if he does not elaborate further on freedom, and maybe this is an omission from the part of the facilitator, the child understands even intuitively the difference that freedom makes to the animals behaviour, even to the environment inside and outside of the cage. These responses seem to align with the findings of Styles and Arizpe's case study (2001) on reading Browne's Zoo to children aged 4-11. They found that children even if not confident yet at reading print, demonstrated impressive capacities for analyzing images.

2) Moments of the dialogue inspired by the questions chosen

Question: Are people animals or not?
Joan: Are we animals?
Facilitator: What do you think?
Joan: I think we are animals. Look the gorilla hides himself and the boy is in the cave and hides himself as well. *(She refers to the page where the child has the strange dream of a child in an animal's cage.)*
Facilitator: Does that similarity makes you think that they are both animals?
Joan: Yes.
Facilitator: What do the others think about that?
Paul: The gorilla hides himself. He is so lonely.
Chris: Maybe he is scared if the people knock the glass (*He refers to the glass around the gorilla's cage*).
Judy(a): He does not have anytime for himself but people have when they are in their houses.
Joan: I think we are animals. Look, children are fighting like animals…mmm the animals don't fight.
Carmen: Yes we are animals. We came from the monkeys and we do things like the monkeys. We eat, climb, walk and mock.
Hilary: The father looks as he has cloud-horns!

Carmen: That's shows he is like an animal.
Loukas: He behaves as an animal. See at the next page, he makes the impression of a gorilla and hits himself.
(Facilitator S. Nikolidaki's log 09/03/2010)

Comments

The first dialogue shows in what ways animals and people are similar. Joan and Carmen argue that people are animals by providing analogical arguments. Therefore, since both gorillas and humans 'eat, climb, walk and mock' they must be both animals. Carmen also gives another argument (of origin) to support her idea that people are animals since they come from monkeys. Unfortunately, this idea was introduced late when it was time to wrap up the session, therefore a good opportunity to explore this idea further was lost. If more time was available the facilitator would ask 'how can we be sure that we come from monkeys?' so as to encourage further Carmen and see whether her answer would refer to some external authority (e.g. my parents told that to me or I read it in the encyclopaedia). Then the discussion would allow others to state their opinions on that idea and possibly the discussion would move to the matter of the origin of species. Even if this discussion never happened, it is necessary for the facilitator and the other members to reflect on the omissions or things that could have happened differently. The wrapping up of the discussion is usually a good time for such reflection so that next time things work better (Gregory, 2007).

Another moment that could have been explored further was Judy's statement about the lack of privacy. It is interesting to see how people's thoughts link together. Paul first wonders about the gorilla's possible loneliness and his hiding. Chris tried to give an explanation for the hiding, therefore he is hypothesising. Judy seems to follow from Chris's ideas and introduces the idea of the constant lack of privacy. It seems that the loneliness that Paul introduced is sometimes desirable as Judy shows with her argument. The facilitator could have picked these ideas and presented them to the other members.

Also, the facilitator could have offered room for hypothetical and creative thinking (thinking upon different premises) by asking the member "How would life be if the walls of our houses were made of glass?" Such a question could have been dealt at both the literal and metaphorical level. However, it is usually hard for the facilitator to think immediately of possible directions that the discussion can take as s/he always has to think 'in situ' (Haynes, 2007; Fisher, 2003).

3) Children and adults dialoguing together.

Observation of the Colours and Shapes of the images

Helen (a): There are always with bright colours the pages with the people but with dark colours the pages that show animals' life. Also the images that show the animals' life follow a particular sequence and the frames are always bigger.

Facilitator: Any idea why this happens?

Loukas: Maybe to show how sad the animals feel *(the shape of the frame shows differences of the emotion!)*

Carmen: Maybe it's just by chance

Loukas: No, can't be. Look *(points at the book)*. It happens all the time. *(Regularity of the action)*

Observation of the black and white pages in the beginning and ending of the book

Hilary: I don't like the ending. It is not happy. It starts with the black and white page and finishes with black and white pages. Why?

Facilitator: Any idea why this happens. Why do we have these two sheets?

Carmen: Maybe they didn't have anything to fill them in so they left them blank

Judy (a): Maybe the white part is the people's feelings and the black is the animals' feelings.

Chris: Mmm maybe that's right. Look the odd pages are for the people and the even for the animals. The odd page is white and the even black! (finds a pattern/argument)

Judy (a): Black and white are not colours. It is the lack of colours so maybe both sides are not either happy or sad.

Hilary: I don't like the end.

Facilitator: Would you like next time to think how you would like the story to end and tell us?

Hilary: Yes!

Comments

Both Helen and Judy (adults) make sophisticated observations, the first one about the use of dark colours when animals' lives are depicted in the pictures and light colours when people's lives in the zoo are portrayed and the second one about what does black and white means in the first and last pages of the book (the contrast in feelings between people- white and animals- black). It is interesting to see Carmen's answer in both cases which are realistic if not nihilistic. Carmen seems to find in both cases non intentionality in the way the certain images have been illustrated. Loukas disagrees in the first dialogue and provides as an argument the frequency that Helen's (adult) observation takes place. Loukas, no matter how young he is, is able to distinguish between incidents that happen on purpose from those happening accidentally. What he attempts is to link cause with effect.

Concluding Discussion

It seems that the community of philosophical inquiry, even at a very early stage, is a place where adults and children's ideas merge together. Both children and adults showed respect for each others' ideas, felt free to link their ideas together, found explanation so as to answer questions that occurred, agreed and disagreed with each other by providing reasons or agreed and found ways to link ideas together (Splitter and Sharp, 1995). Even if this dialogue cannot be characterized as academically philosophical, there is evidence of profound thinking from both adults and children. In many case adults' and children's thinking was critical (e.g. finding examples to support ideas, to agree and to disagree with others) and creative (e.g. when both adults and children associated meaning to the illustration of the book or thought in metaphors).

As for the first question, whether a picture book can give rise to children's and adults' thinking the answer is positive. Picture books are not usually designed for doing philosophy with children, so they lack the 'intentionality' of adding purposefully ideas for the sake of doing philosophy in an academic and often artificial way (Marriott Stuart, 1998). What makes picture books different from intentionally designed stimuli for doing philosophy is that picture books show rather than deliberately tell what might be philosophical. Picture books do not force 'philosophy' but often have 'philosophy' embedded in them. The writer and illustrator Shaun Tan (2009, p.3) claims that "a successful picture book is one in which everything is presented to the reader as a speculative proposition, wrapped in invisible quotation marks, as if to say 'what do you make of this?" This is a form of philosophy that comes not intentionally but one is genuinely interested to find meaning in one's illustration. This is the philosophical thinking that takes place when children reflect on the illustration. When Loukas observed that the grass outside the tiger's cage has more vivid colour than inside and that the tiger has only a 'square' of sky to look at from its cage, then he referred (if not directly) to the value of freedom. His comments certainly made the others think deeply about the illustration and the abstract ideas with which it can be associated with. The silent thinking that takes place in a community of inquiry is as important as the ideas that have been spoken out loud (Haynes, 2007).

The writing of a story reflects the writer's philosophy (the author's thoughts, imagination of how children could think and act, observations as to how children react, and recollection of the child the writer once was (or still is)). The same happens with the reader as beholder and reconstructor of the stimulus in a new way through questioning, inventing new analogies and metaphors, attempting to

understand the writer's initial motivation and pushing thinking into new directions[11].

As for the second question, there are similarities and differences between adults and children in the way they approach and cope with the same stimulus. Children have a more imaginative approach towards the stimulus than the adults. Joan commented on the giraffe licking the paint off the wall because of its thirst, could be ignored or appreciated as 'cute' or 'interesting'. However, Joan's statement has both imagination and logic when Joan elaborated further on her answer. What is important for adults is to really 'listen to the children' and their different approaches because they usually reflect a type of logic which can be impressive.

Children were very able in observing details that could easily have been ignored. Penicillin was discovered because Alexander Fleming was sensitive enough to pay attention to details that others before him had ignored. Genetics also appeared because Mendel was observant enough to identify differences in the colours of the flowers and the shape of the leaves of the varieties of plants that he was cultivating in a monastery. The observation of details can give food to further philosophical investigation and activate both children's and adults' thinking.

Both adults and children ere capable of thinking in metaphors. However, adults could offer more elaborate examples. This could be due to adults' more expanded experiences and more sophisticated use of language. Taking into consideration that most of the adults who contributed were the support workers of the children or some other adults this difference makes sense. Also, both adults and children seemed to pay more attention to

---

[11] Mallan adopts the idea of 'critical aesthetics' which combine the pleasure of reading with practising critique in this reading which seems to describe partly the role between philosophy and literature. Mallan's idea of 'critical aesthetics' is restricted to aesthetics whilst philosophy is broader; it includes aesthetics and does not end in it. (See Mallan,K. 1999. Reading(s) beneath the surface: using picturebooks to foster a critical aesthetics, *Austalian Journal of Language and Literacy*, 22(3), p.200-211).

the information derived from the pictures rather from the text. While I was expecting some comments on the language used in the text, it seemed that the 'power' of the image had the same influence for both adults and children.

The inquiries are still in process. The more adults and children practice their thinking, the more elaborated thoughts they express. Philosophical thinking and wondering does not happen in one example of a case study. It takes time and it lasts as it becomes an attitude of approaching things and thinking on the stimuli received from natural and social environment. Working collaboratively (in groups) and exchanging ideas can only help both adults and children to gain from each other and enhance their understanding. Adults can learn from children's fresh and imaginative approach of a stimulus while children can learn from adults' already experience and ability to state linguistically clearly their ideas and can bust their self esteem as their ideas are appreciated and worthy listening by the adults. Such collaborations between adults and children and combining of their thinking should be encouraged further in the future. Changes in the world happen when all the people's thinking is represented.

Acknowledgments

I would like to thank my supervisor Shirley Egley for her constructive feedback on this paper, Martin Edwards for correcting any grammatical and syntactic mistakes and Caroline McLachlan for enabling me to do this research. Also I would like to thank all the children and adults who participated in my research.

REFERENCES

BROWNE, A. 1994. *Zoo,* London: Red Fox

BURNS, M. M. 1997a. Always popular and sometimes problematic. *Teaching and Learning Literature with Children and Young Adults,* 7(1), pp. 38-47.

BURNS, M. M. 1997b. Sophisticated picture books: An evolving trend for a new age, *Teaching and Learning Literature with Children and Young Adults,* 7(2), pp. 62-71.

EGAN, K. 1988. *Primary Understanding. Education in Early Childhood.* New York: Routledge.

FISHER, R. 2003. *Teaching Thinking, 2nd Edition:*London: Continuum.

GREGORY, M. 2007. A framework for facilitating classroom dialogue, *Teaching Philosophy,* 30(1), pp. 59 - 84.

HAYNES, J. 2002. *Children as philosophers* London: Routledge Falmer.

HAYNES, J. 2007. *Listening as a Critical Practice: Learning from Philosophy with Children,* PhD thesis submitted for examination to University of Exeter.

LIPMAN, M., SHARP, A. M., OSCANYON F. 1980. *Philosophy in the classroom* Philadelphia, PA: Temple University Press.

LIPMAN, M. 1988. *Philosophy goes to School.* Philadelphia: Temple University Press.

LIPMAN, M. 2003. *Thinking in education* (2nd edn) Cambridge & New York: Cambridge University Press.

MARRIOTT, S. 1998. Picture books and the moral imperative, *Paper presented at the British Educational Research Association Annual Conference,Queens University of Belfast, Northern Ireland, August 27th -30th 1998,* pp. 14.

MCCALL, C. 2009. *Transforming Thinking.* London: Routledge

MURRIS, K. 1992. *Teaching Philosophy with Picture Books* (London, Infonet Publications).

NIKOLIDAKI, S. 2010. *Researcher's Log.* Unpublished data.

PIAGET, J.1929. *The Child's Conception of the World.* London: Routledge and Kegan Paul.

REEDER, S.O. 1997. Drawing the line: Defining children's picture books, *Orana* 33 (2), p.20-100.

SCHEINKEMAN,N. 2004. Picturing the story.*Teaching Pre K-8,* 24(6),p.58-59.

SPLITTER, L.J. & SHARP A.M. 1995.*Teaching for better thinking.* Melbourne: ACER

SHAUN, TAN. 2001. Picture books: Who are they for? *Paper presented at the 2001 AATE/ALEA Joint National Conference,* http://www.education.tas.gov.au/curriculum/s tandards/english/english/teachers/discussion/ picture accessed on 10/04/2010.

STYLES, M., ARIZPE, E. 2001. A gorilla with "Grandpa's eyes": How children interpret visual texts. A case study of Anthony Browne's "Zoo", *Children's literature in Education,* 32(4), pp.261-281.

WILLIAMS, S. 2002. Metaphorical Thinking, *Teaching Thinking.* www.teachingthinking.com

WELLER, J. 1984. Sophisticated picture books, *Canadian Library Journal,* 41(1), pp.21-24.

Enhancing Research-Teaching Links in Higher Education
Simon K. Haslett and Hefin Rowlands (eds)
Proceedings of the Newport NEXUS Conference
Centre for Excellence in Learning and Teaching
Special Publication, No. 3, 2010, pp. 31-37
ISBN 978-1-899274-43-7

University of Wales, Newport	Prifysgol Cymru, Casnewydd

Mind the gap: developing flexible learning for professional applications involving law.

Alexandra Dobson and Jo Smedley

Newport Business School, University of Wales, Newport, Allt-yr-yn Campus, Allt-yr-yn Avenue, Newport, NP20 5DA. Email: alexandra.dobson@newport.ac.uk; jo.smedley@newport.ac.uk

Abstract

Developing appropriate flexible learning approaches for the delivery of academic content yields opportunities for increased accessibility on a non-traditional basis. Using a blend of learning styles involving different combinations of modern technologies, materials are available to learners to access on an anywhere-anyhow-anytime basis as they engage with their learning curriculum journey. For traditional academic learners, engaging with non-traditional styles of learning often involves becoming familiar with different types of modern technologies and experiencing different ways of working. For learners who are already work-based and engage with academic learning, the curriculum developments and different styles of learning engagement can present a new type of challenge. Such learners, who are already aware of the practical skills but often seek the theoretical knowledge to broaden their understanding, are an important audience to ensure the currency of the academic learning curriculum. Consequently, their specific needs are a useful natural progression to consider in the development of the modern professional learning experience. This paper considers the pedagogic and practical challenges involved in segmentising a unit of the academic learning curriculum and redesigning the learning experience to attune both to the learners needs and to the requirements of professional/work-based teaching. "Law for Managers", a final year undergraduate 20 credit module, develops knowledge and understanding of managerial responsibilities for a range of legal issues with particular relevance for the workplace, With the aim of providing a range of 'short courses' tailored to the needs of employees who require the tools to identify and analyse legal problems encountered in their place of work, the paper charts the development of discrete 'bite-sized chunks' of learning which can be taught as stand-alone components but which also clearly link with one another to provide a coherent whole learning system. The derivation of each segment is examined in turn with the appropriate learning support elements also discussed. Enabling the accommodation of a range of learner skills and providing graduated approaches to the blended learning experience, these developments enable each short-course/module to be categorised within a blended learning structure to inform subsequent development. An important aspect of the development was to include technologies which were easily accessible and supported the transfer of information, rather than add any considerable learning aspect to the engagement. The specific needs and feedback from the professional learners were gathered at various stages along their learning journey with their comments informing the learning curriculum developments. Finally, this paper proposes a model of learning curriculum development to support the continuing engagement of professional learners with non-traditional learning approaches along a bite-sized learning journey which will link to other subjects within the professional curriculum framework. Recommendations are presented to inform subsequent developments at strategic and operational levels of engagement.

Background

Organisations face challenges in developing leadership and management skills (Senge, 1990, p. 12). In knowledge-based economies, there is a strong interest in increasing the levels of graduate entrepreneurship (Hannon *et al.* 2005). Communities in which entrepreneurship thrive create more jobs and wealth (Formica, 2002). There is a distinctive role for education and universities in the development of wealth and a knowledge based society (Brown *et al.* 2002). The role of higher education in this context is crucial in enhancing the motivation and capability of graduates to engage in entrepreneurial activity. However, if the need for increased levels of graduate entrepreneurship is to be met, it is important to develop more innovative and entrepreneurial approaches during studies. Empowering teams of teachers, students and business people to interact in face-to-face and/or electronic relationships, and to facilitate the formation of networked enterprises emerging from spin-off activities are only a few examples. Educational programs should promote an ethos of lifelong learning and develop in graduates the capacity for long-term personal and professional development through self-learning and reflection. A business degree program should further seek to foster graduates who are confident, creative thinkers with the capacity to solve problems, think creatively, negotiate, make decisions and resolve conflict (Hannon *et al.* 2004). The link between business and technology can never be one to lie dormant for long (Smedley and Svane, 2005). Developing the curriculum further to encompass a still wider range of aspects and concepts shares culture and values and develops and supports people, responding to markets and adding value. The involvement of creative thinkers from industry further enhances the existing curriculum (Pauselli and D'Atri, 2000).

Researching leadership and management needs in organisations

Learning organisations see the major challenges around the recognition of the need for leadership and management development; especially in small and medium enterprises (B2B, 2009). A main challenge for learning organisations and businesses is the demonstration of return on investment, i.e. the measurement of the value of the investment in training and development. An understanding of what business needs in leadership and management training needs a greater understanding and awareness of knowledge of training needs. All too often, training providers see their role in working with businesses to recognise and identify needs, forging partnerships to develop education and development solutions. Subsequent investment is strongly linked to tangible recognition of benefits of improved leadership and management.

The drive for development can be internal in the form of policy and external in the form of business environment. The culture of development tends to come from the top and mid career range staff are generally the target for development. Leadership skills are felt to be needed in relation to business development, general management and personal development. Training budgets range from £25K for the smaller company to £1.3m for those with more than 1000 staff. On average, a quarter to a third of the training budgets are spent on leadership and management development.

Two thirds of organisations have a standard approach across the company to identify staff training needs. Needs are typically established through the vehicle of appraisal/performance reviews with human resource departments who will then have the greatest control in determining the type of training and delivery. Just under a half have a leadership development programme in place which selected staff will follow, and a similar number have a list of approved courses which staff can follow. One in ten allows staff a free choice. Development tends to be directed at first line and middle managers. A range of qualifications are adopted from National Vocational Qualification (NVQ) through to PG qualifications with a fifth using the Institute of Leadership and Management (ILM) and/or Chartered Management Institute (CMI) accredited courses. Most companies adopt a multi method approach to development using a mix of in house and external suppliers, and a range of different learning approaches. Short courses, bespoke courses and coaching are the most common approaches employed. Most staff follow a part-time or distance learning mode of attendance.

Organisations seek flexible delivery blending approaches – online, face to face and work based. They also seek a range of learning approaches to suit different learner styles and access needs (Burgstahler, S., 2010). Work based projects, group activities and presentations, problem based learning, drama, and role play enable a rich mixture of experiences to embed a deeper learning experience. Student evaluation and feedback is required with different assessment approaches for long courses than for short courses. Organisations were less likely to seek external training for these topics than for general management issues such as strategic direction, project management, finance and marketing. Work based projects and flexible delivery are considered the most effective in developing leadership and management skills.

Employers appear to want to be more in the driving seat for leadership and management education and training. There is an appetite for stand alone "build" qualifications, flexibly delivered to suit business demands and needs. Reputation, as well as the offering itself, is critical for suppliers to larger companies. Universities have the equal credibility to deliver in this market with consultants and private providers.

Developing an employer responsive learning curriculum

In this paper the authors chart the development of four short courses derived from a Level 6 Module, 'Law for Managers'. As its name implies the content of this 20-credit module which is offered to full-time and part-time undergraduates studying within Newport Business School is shaped to include areas of law of specific interest to managers. The short courses are some five credits each and are offered through blended learning, with 75% of the teaching offered via distance learning and 25% classroom contact. A description of module content is included later in the paper. As in any worthwhile pedagogic venture the educators have embarked on a journey which has informed their teaching in sometimes unexpected but always enjoyable ways. The short courses are tailored to the needs of the learner in the workplace, and in the process of re-designing what was originally an undergraduate programme, there are a number of challenges. First there is the need to think from the learner's perspective; how, when and where will learning take place? In the traditional undergraduate setting, learners are expected to attend lectures and tutorials in a structured environment. How best to 'mind the gap' and respond to the specific needs of the group of learners by cultivating a conversation (Holmberg, 1989) is central to the exercise.

Within the traditional setting there is an expectation that students will use library facilities and embrace the opportunities for learning support that the University offers, where required. With the non-traditional learner, educators have less guidance to provide the compass points to assist with the journey. Importantly too, the community of learning provided by the panoply of the University may not be available. There is now a body of literature which considers the range of potential barriers (Anderson, 2003) but for the teacher new to this mode of delivery there are pitfalls. Navigating a balanced form of blended learning that provides stimulus, appropriate interaction and access to both the teacher and to fellow learners is not easy. Useful insights into the needs of the professional learner new to law have, however, come from research carried out by Dobson and Marsh (2009) and Dobson (2010) but such research has mainly centred on the needs of part-time students drawn from a particular professional background. It may be however, in the future that aspects of this blended learning delivery will prove appropriate and can be transferred successfully across a number of learning experiences.

Certainly the idea of 'bite sized' accessible chunks of learning delivered flexibly within the workplace or indeed wherever is appropriate for learning to take place is an attractive one. Employers want and often require their employees to gain qualifications whereas employees wish to deepen their knowledge, perhaps with a view to promotion. There is a long history of educational delivery which has used a number of mechanisms to promote learning. Typically in the past, straightforward correspondence courses consisting of hard copies of learning material was used. A prime example of this in law is the University of London's External programme which has allowed law students from all over the world to gain a Bachelor of Laws (LLB). Over the years the material has changed radically moving from the rather 'distant' form of distance learning to a much more personalised service that offers online material combined with intensive study periods at the University. The Open University is another example of an institution that offers a vast range of online resources to support learning and increasingly higher education providers are considering ways of attracting non-traditional learners. How learners learn about law is changing; at a recent Higher Education Academy (HEA) conference, 'Enhancing legal education in Wales' a panel of experts with representatives from the Welsh Assembly Government, the Institute of Legal Executives (ILEX) universities across Wales and a private provider were asked to comment on the future of legal education. It was clear from the discussion that employers are asking for bespoke forms of legal education that fit with the specific needs of the workplace. The delivery strategy underpinning blended learning allows mixed methods of delivery and the question for the teacher is to decide how best to 'blend' the elements to promote effective learning. There are a number of tools to assist the process and with Law for Managers the authors had the advantage of support from the Institute of Digital Learning at the University of Wales, Newport.

The disaggregation process

The first stage in putting together the five credit short courses was to deconstruct the larger module into four accessible blocks of learning. The rationale was that each course could stand alone, thus for instance a short course looking at discrimination or issues of privacy in the workplace would be of use to the learner as a discrete 'bite sized' chunk . Alternatively some learners might choose to study all four of the blocks and by doing this would complete the whole Level 6 module. As flexibility is the key to this mode of learning, the choice over the number and combination of short courses are left to the learner. Taking, 'Discrimination in the Workplace' as an example, the delivery is as follows, contact hours 15, directed study 10 hours and independent study is expected to be some 25 hours. There are six learning outcomes which must be met which span knowledge, argument, communication, contribution and reflection, and practical skills such as referencing. The method of assessment is both formative and summative and here there are some particular challenges but also opportunities which are discussed later in the paper.

Having decided the content of each of the short courses, the next step was crucial. How to translate the content and deliver it to the learner? Translating content in a blended learning environment is dependent on the careful use of resources. Law for Managers is delivered to undergraduates over one semester with some 40 hours contact time. There are a series of lectures and tutorials where complex material is explained and where students are expected to problem solve by considering case studies. Delivery is supplemented by the use of PowerPoint and directed readings which include cases and statutes. With the short course delivery, the use of PowerPoint or some other form of visual aid needed to be rethought. The material would be available via Moodle (a Virtual Learning Environment) and with the more sophisticated range of support systems that come with Moodle it was possible to build in useful aides to learning.

The redesign of the delivery meant that the use of the slides as signposts which provided routes that focused the learner on particular objectives at each stage in the learning journey was crucial. As a pedagogic experiment this reshaping led to a re-assessment of how material can be delivered more generally. Many aspects of the 'signposting' will be incorporated in the undergraduate teaching from October 2010 as a clear advantage of this process was that the delivery of the undergraduate module would also benefit from new approaches that could supplement and enhance the original material. In relation to the design of the resources for the short courses the process was one of trial and error and the objective view provided by the Institute of Digital Learning meant that the educator was encouraged to consider the material from the viewpoint of the learner at each stage. The learner here being one who came into the university at intervals and met with the lecturer and fellow students but who was also required to carry out much of the learning independently. The signposting embedded in the slides typically pointed to links to relevant cases, statutes and key readings but also asked students to carry out certain tasks. These included online discussion through the medium of a forum linked to Moodle, listening to podcasts and watching short films at set intervals. Embedded links to key government websites and to BAILLII, a

website which reports cases, was used as a way of directing students to online resources with the aim of providing a confluence between the limited classroom contact, the online activity and the learning outcomes. Perhaps for the educator embracing new techniques was the greatest challenge. For instance, in producing the podcasts (an Ipod broadcast) there was the need to learn to use Audacity, an online tool that allowed the production of the podcast. Once the practical skills of using the audio system were overcome, a more complex challenge was that of selecting which material to include. The temptation is to use scripted material in a close simulation of a traditional lecture but this is to be avoided as the learning that takes place here is narrow and probably confined to a form of rote learning.

Research discussed by (Hull, 2010) at the Enhancing Legal Education Conference, pointed to students finding limited pedagogic value in this approach, as learner participation was minimal with the learner typically being passive, rather than responsive. Thus the podcasts were kept short and were unscripted and although there was some narrative content, the aim was to use them as guides to support independent learning. How successful they are can only be judged when module feedback is examined in the future. While podcasts can support learning activity and act as a bridge that 'minds the gap' offering a more personalised and informal experience for the learner embarking on blended or distance learning, they provide only one component of the whole. Clearly too, used without other aides to learning, they are potentially discriminatory to those with hearing impairment. Taking into account the shortcomings of podcasts they can stimulate and reinforce learning if used in combination with other tools and are considered appropriate in this context. Vodcasts where a visual image is available in conjunction with audio support is less appropriate here as the learner can utilise the podcast more readily as a form of mobile learning.

A further aid and one which is aligned closely with both the formative and summative assessment is the use of short films presenting students with a range of dilemmas that can arise in the workplace. Again, using film as a teaching medium was a new and stimulating pedagogic method. First appropriate scripts had to be written which would open up lines of discussion and actors were engaged to give the scripts animation. In some ways the scripts mirrored the dilemmas in case studies that undergraduate students are asked to analyse as part of their summative assessment. The films 'added value' by bringing the scenarios to life and will be used as live case studies where students can comment on the online forum but are also asked to debate the issues within class. Clearly there are cost implications in developing a range of resources, such as the ones used in this exercise. The authors are in receipt of a Newport Learning and Teaching Grant, which has been used to develop the materials, and without this it is unlikely that such a full range of resources could have been developed. With the cost implications both in terms of time and money in mind, all the materials have been developed with inbuilt sustainability. For instance, in order that the material remains relevant the scripts have been developed to consider a range of generic themes and thus it is hoped that the dramatised themes will continue to be useful for some time and can be used across a range of learning experiences. Within the short courses they will be used as a feature of the formative assessment which in turn will assist with the summative group presentation and linked written assignment, where students are asked to consider a range of legal issues and provide advice to a fictional client.

While both the use of the podcasts and the films is an important tool in creating a link between the distance element of the learning and classroom contact, learners will also be provided with 'workbooks' at induction that supplements the material available on moodle. The overarching aim is to provide a diverse range of pedagogic resources which provide support and promote inclusivity. Each short course' is provided with the full range of learning support with the emphasis on accessibility combined with an expectation that if used fully the material will enhance a rigorous academic learning experience.

Lessons learned

Deconstructing an existing module and then rebuilding and shaping the segments to fit new learners in a blended learning environment is demanding and requires a form of 'pedagogic negotiation' which is reliant on the educator being prepared to embrace new ideas. It is time-consuming, as the new ideas must be carefully considered and there is constantly the need to consider the teaching and the supporting material from the learner's perspective. Of course, all good pedagogic undertakings should commence with a clear view of the needs of the learner but where a module is already in existence, it is tempting to see the process as one of rearrangement. In order to tailor the material and truly 'blend' learning a simple reconfiguration is inadequate. Changing from a traditional form of teaching to something which embraces novel techniques requires a re-alignment on the part of the educator which is sometimes unsettling. Placed alongside this however, the new aspects of the courses have opened a new range of possibilities that the authors intend to explore further. Clearly caution has to be exercised as some of the 'new' facilities such as the use of podcasts are useful but can be of limited effect if used without care. It might also be argued that they are simply a reinvention of techniques used in the past but there is merit it is suggested in providing such support where the learner may otherwise feel distanced from the University. At the time of writing the expectation is that the learner is situated in 'a' workplace but the courses have been developed in order that they can be relevant to managers in a range of workplace environments. It is likely that once teaching commences fine tuning may have to take place to take into account specific needs and particular environments. Further as with any pedagogic venture, it is or should be, a continuing journey both for the learner and for the educator.

REFERENCES

ANDERSON, 2003. Getting the mix right again: An updated and theoretical rationale for interaction. *The International Review of Research in Open and Distance Learning*, 4 (2), www.irrodl.org/index.php/iirodl/article/view/149/230 retrieved 4.4.10

B2B INTERNATIONAL, 2010. *Market Research Report for University of Wales, Newport.*

DOBSON, A. 2010. *The Challenges and Opportunities of Contextualising Legal Education: Learning in Law.* Annual Conference, Higher Education Academy, Warwick University (January 2010)

DOBSON, A., MARSH, T. 2008. Learning the Law: a pilot study examining challenges facing non-law students studying law. *Newport CELT Journal*, 1, pp. 23-28.

BROWN, R. A., PUDDICK, R. 2002. Experiencing entrepreneurship at Cambridge. *Industry and Higher Education*, 16 (1), pp. 49-53.

BURGSTAHLER, S. (2010) *Real Connections: Making Distance Learning Accessible to Everyone* http://www.washington.edu/doit/Brochures/Technology/distance.learn.html accessed 2.4.10

FORMICA, P. 2002. Entrepreneurial Universities. *Industry and Higher Education*. 16(3), pp. 167-175.

HANNON, P., COLLINS, L.A., SMITH, A.J. 2005. Exploring graduate entrepreneurship. *Industry and Higher Education*, 19(1), pp. 11-23.

HANNON, S., MCBRIDE, H., BURNS, B. 2004. Developing creative and critical thinking abilities in business graduates: the value of experiential thinking techniques. *Industry and Higher Education,* 18(2), pp. 95-100.

HOLMBERG, B. 1989. *Theory and Practice of Distance Education.* Routledge. http://www.londonexternal.ac.uk/current_students/programme_resources/laws/llb_diplaw/llb.shtml accessed 4.4.10

HULL, C. 2010. Presentation at *Enhancing Legal Education in Wales* Conference, UK Centre for Legal Education (Higher Education Academy). University of Glamorgan, April 2010.

PAUSELLI, E., D'ATRI, A. 2000. Distance learning for SME Managers. *Industry and Higher Education,* 15(2) pp. 117-123.

SENGE, P. 1990. The Fifth Discipline: The Art and Practice of The Learning Organisation. Doubleday, New York.

SMEDLEY, J.K., SVANE, T. 2005. *Getting down to business*, Proceedings of ITHET 2005 Conference, Dominican Republic, July 2005.

University of Wales, Newport

Prifysgol Cymru, Casnewydd

Enhancing Research-Teaching Links in Higher Education
Simon K. Haslett and Hefin Rowlands (eds)
Proceedings of the Newport NEXUS Conference
Centre for Excellence in Learning and Teaching
Special Publication, No. 3, 2010, pp. 38-47
ISBN 978-1-899274-43-7

Exploring the impact of coaching cultures on the professional development and self-actualisation of academic identities in Higher Education Institutions.

Jo Maddern

Centre for the Development of Staff and Academic Practice, Aberystwyth University, SY23 3DD.
Email: oam@aber.ac.uk

Abstract

Whilst there is ample evidence of the effectiveness of coaching in the sports and business arena, coaching in Higher Education is a newer phenomenon, one not yet fully embedded or accepted. A strong current evidence-base of research showing its efficacy is yet to be developed by researchers, yet strong anecdotal evidence suggests that the further development of cultures of coaching in Higher Education could be enormously beneficial in helping academics reconcile the often conflicting demands (of teaching, research and administration) they are faced with as well as optimising their performance, increasing productivity and helping them achieve their goals. It is argued by the author that the complexities of performing academic identities in contemporary society necessitates some kind of coaching environment for optimum performance, work/life satisfaction and productivity. This paper lays out the ongoing and emergent research of the author, which uses an action – research methodology to examine the impacts of coaching in Higher Education Environments.

Introduction: Coaching 'Ecosystems' in Higher Education

'Let me state why I think coaching is important. Coaching has the capacity to bring humanity back into the workplace. This is critical because much of what we are doing in the workplace - and beyond – has the effect of squeezing humanity out. The ever increasing drive for efficiencies (not effectiveness, note), the restructuring, the re-engineering, the ever more stretching goals, the apparent expendability of the 'human resource', all these, unfettered, sap spirit, energy and creativity and thus impoverish the human being and the organization in which they work. But even despite all that, if we are able to take the opportunity offered to us right now, we will realize that we are… on the brink of discovering the extraordinary

benefits of letting humanity loose in the workplace – and beyond. When the whole human being, with all its capacities – intelligence, creativity, imagination, sensitivity and pragmatism to name but a few… expresses itself in the workplace, then extraordinary results accrue' (Downey, 2003, x-xxi).

You all live within your own 'ecosystems', joked the highly successful executive coach, Thomas Preston, as I sat in a seminar and talked about issues of value and pricing in the coaching world (Tom's work has led him to coach individuals from some of the world's most successful business and highest net worth families). The impact of coaching could be 'priceless' we concluded, if it meant that people could realize their deepest dreams of fulfil their most cherished professional ambitions. 'Priceless', has two meanings attached – beyond simple economic value, but also incredibly hard to put a value on – and therein lies the problem with trying to put a simple quantitative value onto the 'magic' that seems to happen in coaching encounters and how that can be 'made to work' in the university environment. This made incredible sense. I loved the 'ecosystem' description Tom used, partly because of my background as a geographer, but also because it was such a rich, accurate description of the uniqueness and interrelatedness of the Higher Education 'communities of practice' (we all live and work, thrive or fail to thrive in, as well as the variation in the way that coaching is 'valued' within that particular ecosystem). Ecosystems are co-assemblages of plants and animals, and non 'living' structures such as soils and climate. The metaphor of an ecosystem can quite easily be used to describe the human and non-human environments we as academics have to make decisions about 'research' and 'teaching' and how we make sense of the relatedness between the two. Yet it is crucial to understand how important human relationships are to the achievement of excellence within any organization, not least Higher Education, which is about learning and development as a core value. It is the relationships between people that largely enable teaching and research excellence to occur. However, until now, with a few 'good practice' exceptions, the human relatedness aspect of performance in HE have largely remained unexamined and taken for granted in many institutions until now. This paper will examine the good practice case studies gathered from a range of HE institutions, as a way of making a case for the use of coaching as a way of maximizing performance at the interface of teaching and research.

The impact of coaching has long been recognized in the business world, where Return on Investment (ROI) studies are able to provide something of a solid, quantitative evidence base for the positive economic as well as social impact coaching has. Consider these figures, which measure both 'soft' (intangible) and 'hard' (economic gain) indicators ROI from executive coaching at several well known multinational corporations:

- 761 executives from Dell Computers received coaching for two years. Feedback forms demonstrated a 90% satisfaction rate from executives coached. Research showed that the 'coached' executives were, on average much more likely to receive promotions than non-coached colleagues.

- A poll of mostly fortune 1,000 companies suggested that participants valued coaching at six times the cost paid by their company, so, an $18,000 programme investment generated value at approximately $108,000

- A survey of Metric Global 's 43 leadership development participants suggested that coaching delivered an ROI of 5.7 times the initial investment. The benefits perceived included: productivity increases (53%), customer service improvements (39%), executive retention (32%), supervisor relationship improvements (over 70%) and job satisfaction (52%).

- Tom Preston & Associates Executive Coaching Specialists, who work with hundreds of international firms including Danone, Citigroup, Dyson Limited and Yo! Sushi, estimate an average ROI from executive coaching programs to be not less than 20 times initial coast of coaching programs provided (from a combination of individual and team coaching). Source: Tom Preston and Associates (2010).

These and other ROI studies have led to the generally uncontested acceptance of executive coaching as a way to improve performance within business. Of course, the ROI methodology itself has had a variable reputation, but since the object of analysis is human capital, with all the messy complexities that entails, soft, qualitative data must be combined with 'hard', economic analysis for the truest picture.

Characteristically, an organisation where a coaching culture exists is one where coaching is linked into strategic objectives, not seen as a stand-alone solution to all development needs. The CIPD's (Chartered Institute of Personnel and Development) 2007 learning and development survey suggested that 71% of organisations now use coaching as a learning and development tool. However, results from the survey indicated wide variations in practice to develop a coaching culture, with clear objectives in relation to coaching being rare at senior management level.

Despite these compelling statistics, coaching effectiveness has taken longer to gain a theoretical purchase in the academy, where it has long been presupposed that 'talent' and 'good ideas' will speak and act for themselves. It is no surprise then, that coaching has largely been 'normalized' as leading to improved performance in the business world, yet remains more marginal in HE.

In fact, a solid evidence-base for the impact of coaching in HE has yet to be developed, a gap which this research project seeks to address, through a mixed methods approach that includes a quantitative (return on investment or 'ROI') methodology, exploration of good practice case studies collected from across the United Kingdom and through collecting the narratives of those who coach and are coached within Higher Education in the twenty-first century. This is by no means a finished piece of work, but rather, a set of 'initial thoughts' that act as a starting point for the gathering of empirical coaching narratives. Alongside economic indicators, the life-narratives of academics as they make integrated decisions about what to research, how to research it, what to teach and how to teach it, within the departmental and institutional 'ecosystems' they inhabit will be collected, to provide empirical depth to the impact of coaching on teaching and research performance in HE.

In fact, it may be argued that the rolling out of 'coaching cultures' in HE and the researching of those cultures are crucial in a climate of heightened and accelerated change. Indeed, some work has already been done, yet gaps remain. In her work on the strategic leadership of change in Higher Education, Marshall argues that '… the process of leadership development must be closely interwoven with storytelling within organizations' 2007, xx). Similarly, Harding (2009) has examined action research approaches, grounded theory perspectives and a case study approach as methodologies suitable for research into coaching in HE, through her research into how coaching and mentoring is being used to support the alignment of academic staff and institutional strategy during a period of significant change in university in the South of England.

To reiterate, this research, whilst in its nascent stage, uses a case study approach, which interweaves qualitative narratives and good practice studies. Through these rich narratives, different typologies of coaching emerge, each of which are explored systematically. Attention is given to:

- The impact of women-women coaching as part of pan university schemes addressing the underrepresentation of women at senior management levels;
- The use of peer coaching systems, coaching cultures and management styles infused with coaching consciousness or what we might call 'the art of appreciative enquiry';
- Top management tier coaching, (sometimes leading to that increasingly well known condition, 'coaching envy' amongst the rest of the of the university populace);
- Remedial coaching (where it is bought in as a last resort by Human Resources departments when individuals are underperforming or causing disharmony in their immediate environments);
- Coaching for excellence in teaching and research;
- Coaching students towards employability and personal development as part of personal tutoring systems.

Taken as a whole, it is hoped that these case studies will present compelling evidence that coaching should be embedded across *all* levels of an institution, for it to gain maximum 'return on investment' and to allow the institution, to begin to reach its maximum level of creativity and excellence, and for those within it to become as 'self-actualised' professionals (and human beings) as possible.

Who moved my mortarboard?

Things are changing rapidly in universities. Higher Education institutions have long existed with an 'ivory tower' mentality, unconcerned about the latest leadership and management trends and 'fads' in the business world and in fact, wearing this isolationist stance as a badge of honour and neutrality. However, a number of changes have meant that to survive, universities must increasingly 'think' like businesses and engage with market forces, like other sectors of commerce. As Race (2010) puts it:

"In the UK, and in many other countries, higher education is already being 'squeezed' and faces the prospect of very significant and ongoing reductions in funding in the next few years. There is, however, a lot we can do to improve the quality of teaching, learning and assessment in higher education without spending more money or time"[1]

Maximizing the 'return on people employed' (what, Tomas Preston calls 'ROPE'), is one way to improve quality, and it argues that coaching an effective avenue to achieve this in HE. The global economic recession has added the most recent layer of pressures yet; pressures of various kinds have been accumulating in Higher Education for at least the last two decades. The top down, governmental push to 're-professionalize' academic staff, the introduction of students as fee paying 'consumers' and increasing culture of 'audit' and 'quality' assessment have all left their imprint in the working lives of academics, in fact, weaving their way subtly through their everyday lives, behaviours, practices and habits, at home and at work. Choices made by academics must 'ride the waves' of national and local changes, whilst retaining a sense of independence and autonomy. Clegg, for instance, suggests that, Universities are now super-complex environments. Her ideas are worth quoting at length:

"Universities and academic life are becoming more complex and differentiated spaces. Barnett (1999, 2000, 2003, 2005) has described these elements in terms of 'super-complexity' and he, along with many others, has analysed the tendencies towards a fracturing of the presumed unity between teaching and research (Barnett, 2003, 2005). Governments internationally are driven by the twin concerns of global competitiveness and the need to produce local, flexible, employable workers as part of supply side neo-liberal economic strategies… they are also pursuing this project while simultaneously in developed nations at least, de-investing in student support by shifting the financial burden onto students and their parents… Highly selective increased research funding strategies … are being pursued alongside a widening participation, supply side strategy based on reducing unit cost. This has major ideological consequences in disarticulating what were perceived to be radical projects… such as increased access and reformed pedagogical approaches, creating in their wake what Barnett (2003) has described as a series of pernicious ideologies. Not least of these pernicious ideologies is that of quality and audit. Numerous writers have described the seemingly malign influence of managerialist practices… and consumerism, in undermining the traditional autonomy and respect accorded to academics as intellectuals and professionals in the Schönian sense" (Clegg, 2006, 303).

---

[1] http://phil-.co.uk/, 3/2/2010

Clegg's paper suggests that academics face less time where they are able to 'reflect' as professionals, due to the rise of 'super-complexity'. Yet Schonian reflection is crucial to the academic-identity-project and the integration of research and teaching identities into a self-fulfilling work-life project. The description of 'super-complexity' is an apt one. As these supra-national policies trickle down and manifest themselves in the day-to-day realities of academic working lives, the case for coaching becomes a compelling one. The irony of this is that, despite the protestations of administrative staff regarding the puff-chested, sometimes arrogant and disorganized person they feel they have to 'manage', academics are in fact, generally sensitive individuals that need their 'creature comforts' in place to thrive and survive (creatures comforts that are sometimes hard to come by in the 1960s structures that suffice as offices and lecture halls). It is the many social, economic and political forces working on and through them, combined with their intellects that produce these 'identities'. The notion of academics needing 'talent management' has gained currency amid these sometimes stifling changes. This has led to the increasing notion of 'talent management' as being crucial to the success of a Higher Education. Indeed, leadership and change experts Goffee and Jones (2009) identify a breed of individuals they call 'Clevers', individuals which exist in many sectors.

'We found value-creating brilliance in a huge variety of places… Without clever people, leaders cannot hope to succeed. Without good leadership, Clevers can never realize their full potential. They are in it together. Clevers need leaders; and leaders need Clevers. And both need organizations. Together they can achieve great things. But one without the other will fail' (2009, XVII).

Thus, the authors argue that the relationship between leaders and led is symbiotic and not hierarchical. They suggest that certain conditions are needed for clever individuals to flourish: 'organised space' for their creativity, leaders that tell them what to do, but not how to do it, management structures that can 'sense' the needs of clever people and keep them motivated, places and situations where they can connect with 'clever' peers and a conviction that a larger organization is central to their success (these are all qualities that a coaching culture can provide). Thus, cleverness does not exist, or at least become effectitiously productive within a vacuum. Clevers need fertile soil to flourish and become what they are meant to be. Clevers, we might argue, are rather like sunflowers, which are brilliant and dazzling, yet cannot grow and thrive without the right ingredients – constant support, sun, a rich, fertile environment and regular hydration. This stands in opposition to the notion of a 'tall poppy', ruggedly individualist, with a fine stem, blowing in the breeze, ready to be cut down at any moment, by a competitive colleague, inside the institution. You might recognize these 'sunflowers' in your institution – you might even be one. Higher Education institutions are, I would argue, full to bursting with 'sunflowers', yet, it could be argued that more attention needs to be paid to the pressures that these individuals face, the new ecosystems and the environments that they live within and a coaching culture developed to work with these pressures, in order to gain maximum 'sunflower growth' or 'return on people employed' (ROPE).

We are not yet leaving the arena of 'nature' metaphors, in fact they are highly productive (sic) for thinking about the benefits of coaching in universities, since Universities, and by their nature are places of growth through interaction. The work of Goffee and Jones (2009) has strong resonances with the work of Nancy Klein (1999) who has developed the idea of the 'Thinking Environment'. Kline (2009) details ten components of the 'thinking environment', which includes the quality of the place we inhabit, the ability for those within it to listen actively and act as 'thinking partners', and the ability for others to ask 'incisive questions' which help to pierce limiting beliefs. Much like fertile conditions for the sunflower – the quality of 'growing' we are able to do in an organization depends on the quality of the environment we are placed within and the quality of 'listening', crucially, that takes place within those ecosystems. As Kline puts it, emphatically,

'The Thinking Environment is natural, but rare. It has been squeezed out of our lives and organizations by inferior ways of treating each other. Organizations, families, relationships can become Thinking Environments again, where good ideas abound and, action follows and people flourish' (2005, 13).

In some ways we are better off in universities than much of the business world and in some ways, much worse. Two discourses or 'ways of being' circulate around our contemporary institutions, and spaces of higher education. Go to any international conference and you are likely to see plenty of 'active listening', appropriately incisive questioning (at the right time, and not before) and rapt attention, what we might call 'appreciative enquiry'. However, visit a staff room at coffee time, or a departmental meeting in an average department where the subject is departmental strategy, and you are likely to see lots of talking, but perhaps not so much active listening, and often a top-down approach to decision making. This is erroneous, given that Goffee and Jones (2009) suggest that Clevers, to flourish, can be told broadly what do, but not the finer details of how to do it. That is where their brilliance and creative flair ignites itself (brilliance that is at the heart of the research-teaching nexus). I am arguing that we have stopped properly listening to each other in universities. At least, we stopped the kind of rich, active listening that Kline advocates, the kind of listening and 'appreciative enquiry' that allows people to 'think for themselves'. This is important Kline suggests, because 'everything we do depends on the thinking we do first' and 'our thinking depends on the quality of our attention for

each other'. I also propose a self-conscious return to a proper 'appreciative enquiry' within the spaces of the 'academe', perhaps a turn that has never been needed before as much as it is now, given the global recession and funding cut-backs facing most higher education institutions today. Indeed, it has been shown by well-respected 'stress experts' such as John Perry, that stressors in the working environment can reduce IQ by up to 20 points (and additionally, can allow, what Damien Hughes, author of 'Liquid Thinking' calls, regressive 'chimp' like behaviour to come to the forefront, shutting down the more evolved parts of our brain concerned with reasoning and intellectual functions). Given that universities are a major part of the 'knowledge economy', this should be of immediate concern to senior management and academic developers. For us to do our best, most brilliant thinking about how we research and how we teach, we need to be in a relaxed state, with a receptive and appreciative audience. As Kline suggests, *'perhaps the most important thing we could do with our life and with our leadership is to listen to people so expertly, to give them attention so respectfully they would begin to think for themselves, clearly and afresh'* (2005, 17).

The kind of rugged sparring we have come to know as a hallmark of academic life, may work well in the spaces of discipline-based subject enquiry (when counterbalanced by a community of disciplinary belonging and 'in it together mentality'), but not in the every-day planning and management spaces of the academic world. It an irony that whilst purposeful thinking has long been the linga franca of university life, modern pressures such as performance targets, managerialism, re-professionalisation, increasing student fees and soft and hard funding capping by funding bodies such as HEFCW and HEFCE, universities are harder places to 'think' clearly and creatively in than ever before.

Thus, this paper foregrounds empirical research that makes the case for the development of Universities with coaching cultures at their heart, a culture that is not free floating, but linked to strategic objectives.

What is Coaching?

An organisation's definition of coaching must be congruent with the existing culture and language of that organisation. Like any 'emergent' discipline however, the boundaries and borders of coaching are still being defined. Rather than seeing this as a negative thing, it is in fact an opportunity for exciting change, since, as many geographers, multicultural and postcolonial theorists have argued, it is often at the 'borders' that the most innovative things happen. There are then, several models of coaching, often stemming from the different psychotherapeutic traditions they are usually embedded within. What is consistent among these approached is that coaching is solution-focused and resolutely present and future-focused (rather that the problem and past orientated approaches, which are, nevertheless extremely relevant in deeper psychological cases of need such as addiction or mental-health cases). The above quote exemplifies the approach of coaching, of starting where the 'client is at' temporally as well as psychologically. The client is not seen as 'broken' and so the coach does not try to 'fix' them. Clients are seen as resourceful individuals able to find the solutions to their own changes, given the right environment, which a talented coach is able to provide. Whilst the therapist might march off into the childhood looking for causes for current issues, the coach does not presuppose such a relationship (though they will be open to this if one emerges). That is what makes coaching distinctive from other 'talking' and 'listening' 'therapies', if indeed we may call it a therapy at all.

Furthermore, we might imagine a continuum of coaching approaches, with on the one hand, the 'non-directive' approach favoured by Nancy Kline, a tradition that stems from the Carl Rogers school of psychotherapy, where the focus is active listening and minimal 'intervention' by the coach. The extreme other end of the spectrum

is the very directive, challenging coach, who engages in more active 'interventions' and more tough questioning. In between these two extremes exists a range of methods and approaches. Mentoring, for example, blends the championing, goal setting and support of coaching with 'advice' and 'guidance' of an individual mentor drawing on their expertise in the area the 'mentee' is concerned with developing. Passmore (2006) defines the difference between coaching and mentoring as follows:

"A mentor has experience in a particular field and imparts specific knowledge, acting as adviser, counsellor, guide, tutor, or teacher. In contrast, the coach's role is not to advise but to assist coachees in uncovering their own knowledge and skills and to facilitate coachees in becoming their own advisers."

Similarly, a consultancy approach with blend motivational techniques and active listening with an 'advice-based' approach. Other approaches include Behavioural change approaches such as 'neuro-linguistic programming, time-line work *etc*, which are based on a behavioural–cognitive change model.

Perhaps the most effective method, we might argue is the non-directive approach to coaching, where people are encouraged to 'think for themselves'. Nancy Kline was developed this approach over twenty years ago, after she founded a school in the US. She noticed that the single most important factor in the quality of people's thinking was the way they were being treated by those around them. She noticed that when the components of the thinking environment were in place, school children's' IQ seemed to increase, and behavioural problems subside. She went on the lay out the ten qualities of a thinking environment (Figure 1). This kind of environment where high level thinking is possible can be created by two people, a group or any other type of meeting.

Taken collectively, the components of a 'thinking environment', Kline argues, create high performance teams and individuals who can 'think for themselves'. Given that HEIs rate individual thinking as a key attribute, then the creation of a Nancy Kline style thinking environment, it is argued could be the setting in which the research-teaching nexus can most clearly unfold.

Developing Coaching Cultures in HE

'Coaching is the predominant style of managing and working together, and where a commitment to grow the organisation is embedded in a parallel commitment to grow the people of the organisation' (Clutterbuck and Megginson, 2005).

There are a number of UK institutions in which coaching has been successfully embedded on a cultural level. The two boxes below show 'good practice' case studies from Wolverhampton University and Leeds Metropolitan University, where recent initiatives to take on a culture of coaching have been successfully embedded:

Case study 1: University of Wolverhampton

The University brings in professional coaches for its Senior and Managerial staff. In addition, the Staff Mentoring Scheme, which is funded by the Equality and Diversity Unit within the university, utilises external trained coaches who work in the university and also trains staff mentors from within the organisation. The Staff Mentoring Scheme provides mentoring for all staff in all tiers and sectors of the institution. The scheme also actively encourages participation by minority staff who may shy away from mentoring, thinking it is not suitable for their needs. The Staff Mentoring Scheme provides all staff with the opportunity to engage in self identified professional development. In time, it is anticipated that mentoring will positively impact of the progression of staff within the university. Mentees have approached the scheme for many forms of professional development including performance enhancement, conflict resolution, improving working relationship, improving communication with colleagues, developing management and leadership skills, improving research skills, improving learning and teaching skill and career progression. Evaluations of the programme indicate that the scheme aids improvements in all of these areas. Evaluations of the scheme have taken place and reveals reported benefits beyond professional development. The scheme was reported to be both useful and valuable. Staff felt that mentoring was useful as it is inspirational, encourages networking and skills development and increases diversity of thought and productivity. The scheme was found valuable as it lead to skills and career enhancement, helped new and existing staff, provides emotional support, led to staff feeling valued by colleagues and the institution, led to greater levels of job satisfaction, impacts positively on professionalism, increases productivity and encourages staff to engage in more activities that enhanced the Institution's reputation. As a result, staff requested that the scheme becomes a permanent strategy for Staff Development. Further research has also indicated that staff involved in mentoring feel that it impacts positively on work related stress levels, in emotional, cognitive and behavioural ways. Mentors report that mentoring is beneficial as it encourages them to feel valued within the organisation, provides them with diversity in strategies for dealing with stress and provides the opportunity to reflect. Mentees suggest that mentoring helps them feel more confident in the work place, provides diverse strategies for coping in the work place and provides the opportunity for reflection.

We have attempted to create a coaching culture by instituting a formal mentoring scheme, which has an identified and funded coordinator, through providing training, CPD and Supervision for its mentors. As a result, the scheme provides a highly professional and effective mentoring for the institution's staff. Workload allocation has been negotiated for those involved in the scheme to encourage staff mentors and mentees to prioritise their mentoring relationship and activities. The scheme has a good reputation within the institution and this has encouraged and enhanced participation.

For more information, contact: Dr Debra Cureton, Mentoring and Coaching Development Research Fellow, University of Wolverhampton, d.cureton@wlv.ac.uk, telephone 01902321293.

Case Study 2: Leeds Met Coaching Strategy

"The development of coaching within Leeds Met is essential to realise Vision and Character, foster "talents to the full", support the scale of change envisaged across the University, and to support implementation of the new Performance Development Review system. It will enhance the aims of the ACTs framework, such as improved performance, increased motivation, empowerment, and skills development. The 2008 Staff Development Festival had as its theme "Coaching with a difference", which further emphasised Leeds Met as viewing coaching as crucial to its core business, following the University's recent award as the UK Centre for Coaching Excellence.

Figure 1: Nancy Kline's Thinking Environment.

The benefit of introducing coaching to the organisation links in with the overarching aim of Leeds Met Acts – "to attract, retain, develop and promote staff with the attitude to make a difference…." Organisations who have introduced coaching have outlined some of the following benefits:

- more effective leadership
- reduced sickness absence
- increased productivity
- improved outcomes
- a workforce better equipped to manage change
- greater job satisfaction
- more motivated workforce

These extracts are just parts of a much larger set of documents, but give interesting insights into the ways in which coaching is being thought about as part of academic lives. Coaching is not only a lens through which research-teaching nexus issues can be captured and visualized, it is also a medium through which professional development and self-actualization of individual academics can occur – whereby these two, sometimes competing strands of academic life can be reconciled. I have seen firsthand the positive impact coaching can have in terms of an individual's confidence to teach, as I have 'coached' individuals on the Postgraduate Certificate of Teaching in HE programme at Aberystwyth University. This research seeks to add empirical depth and rigour to anecdotal accounts.

Conclusions

As the case studies above illustrate, many universities are seeing the benefits of adopting a coaching culture in teaching, research and management. Whilst return on investment studies do exist, what is lacking is procedural insight into the thinking patterns of academics as they are coached to make decisions regarding their research and teaching lives. This is by no means a finished piece of work, indeed it is only the start of a much larger research project that seeks to 'collect' and document the life-narratives of academics as they are coached and make decisions about research, teaching and academic practice. By doing this, a much clearer picture will form of the contextual, affectual and reasoned decisions are made by academic-identities in the integration of the research-teaching nexus into their own professional subjectivities as part of their developmental projects.

REFERENCES

CLEGG, S. 2008. Academic identities under threat? *British Educational Research Journal,* 34 (3), pp. 329-345.

CLUTTERBUCK, MEGGINSON 2005. How to create a coaching culture. *People Management,* 11 (8), 21 April, pp. 44-45.

DOWNEY, M. 2003. *Effective Coaching: Lessons from the coaches' coach.* United Kingdom. Cengate Learning.

GOFFEE, R., JONES, G. 2009. *Clever: Leading your smartest, most creative people.* Boston: Harvard Business Press.

HARDING, C. 2009. A methodology that is just right for a coaching research study. *International Journal of Evidence Based Coaching and Mentoring,* Special Issue No 3, pp. 14–21.

HUGHES, D. 2009. *Liquid Thinking.* Capstone Publishing.

KLINE, N. 2009. *Time to Think: Listening to Ignite the Human Mind.* London, Cassell Illustrated.

PASSMORE, J. 2009. Coaching ethics: making ethical decisions: experts and novices. *The Coaching Psychologist.*

PRESTON, T. 2000. *Coach Yourself to Success.* London: Management Books.

Enhancing Research-Teaching Links in Higher Education
Simon K. Haslett and Hefin Rowlands (eds)
Proceedings of the Newport NEXUS Conference
Centre for Excellence in Learning and Teaching
Special Publication, No. 3, 2010, pp. 48-52
ISBN 978-1-899274-43-7

University of Wales, Newport

Prifysgol Cymru, Casnewydd

Developing a practice-led methodology for a photographic PhD.

John Paul Spooner

32 Windsor Drive, South Hetton, County Durham, DH6 2UU. Email: paulyspooner@hotmail.com

Abstract

The following describes the strategy for the development of a practice-led photography PhD project. The research is intended to disentangle the historical and contemporary perceptions of the British new town in order to explore their legacy of unattained utopian idealism. The project will examine the role of photography as a means by which the chronology of new town development can be scrutinised in a way that highlights the stratification of urban history resulting from subsequent phases of new town development. This paper will detail the processes involved in forming a framework from which to conduct useful, and tangible, research results by discussing the influences and theories that have informed my practice.

Introduction

My purpose in writing this paper is to address, in general terms, the processes I have undergone in order to develop a coherent methodology for the pursuit of a practice-led photographic PhD. I also hope to highlight the way in which this process has enabled me to engage in my own pedagogical development.

This paper is perhaps not the traditional kind of document you might expect to be delivered at a conference dealing with pedagogy. For a start, it is not about teaching per-se, but about learning – and in particular the way in which my own learning journey has progressed as I work towards my goal of achieving a PhD.

Teaching is not completely ignored – having been a tutor for almost ten years, teaching has always been part of my practice as a photographer, and will be an even larger part of this practice as I undertake a PGCE in September in order to teach the new Creative and Media Diploma.

With this in mind, the following paper should be seen through the lens of a personal learning journey – one which I hope will stand me in good stead in my future teaching career, and will also enable me to achieve my PhD.

I have been a photographer for 17 years. Following a 1st Class honours degree from Sunderland University in 2001, I gained a Masters Degree in photography in 2002, also at Sunderland. Following this I began an M-phil research degree in 2003 at The University of Wales, Newport, from which I successfully transferred to a PhD in 2006. Shortly thereafter, I took an extended sabbatical, returning to my study in late 2009.

Chronology

From their beginnings in the Arts and Crafts Movement of the early 20th century, new towns have helped shape our urban landscape by providing a test bed for all manner of architectural experiments. From Formalism to Modernism, Structuralism to Postmodernism, and finally to De-constructivism, new towns have been the proving ground for many of the architectural styles that still shape our towns and cities today.

In 1923, Le Corbusier described a house as "a machine for living in", *(Vers une Architecture, 1923.)* This modernist philosophy is reflected in subsequent new town development, culminating in some strikingly modernist architectural elements in the last generation of new towns.

The roots of this Modernist Movement can be traced back to social and technological changes at the end of the 19th century, as in the west cities were expanding thanks to new approaches to building and new technologies, which allowed cheaper and more efficient means of housing a growing population.

In America, the architect Louis Sullivan coined the phrase "form follows function", *("The Tall Office Building artistically considered"," Lippincott's Magazine, March 1896)* as he and his contemporaries developed the iconic skyscraper. The response of European architects to the American advances would lead to the development of Modernism in Europe.

In modernist town planning the emphasis was upon rationalism, prompting planners to come up with the idea of Comprehensive Redevelopment Areas, *(Town and Country Planning Act (1947).* The approach involved demolishing existing infrastructure in order to arrive at a blank slate from which the city could be rationally planned afresh.

New towns share a contentious place in the collective consciousness. Often viewed as anachronisms from an age of forgotten utopian idealism, far from representing a single period in the history of urban design, new towns have complex chronologies that reflect much broader changes in urban design. My interest lies in the application of practice-led photographic research as a means by which this chronology can be examined.

Developing a methodology

When I began my research my practice as a photographer was firmly established in the documentary tradition, but was slowly developing into one more contingent with contemporary landscape photographic practice.

Previously, my strengths as a photographer were in my practice. Understanding of critical context had always been an important part of my work, but at an undergraduate level the practical application of photography tends to dominate the contextual.

Typically a project would stem from an initial idea, an interest in a particular topic or an interesting piece of information; this would then provoke a photographic response, resulting in a series of images that would in some way reinforce the initial idea.

Whilst this an ideal approach to traditional documentary photography, in order to produce original research to support a PhD, a different methodology must be followed.

Having already done some work on my research topic at MA level, I had a general idea of the projects I wanted to pursue, but my overall aims were still somewhat undefined, which is where the process of developing a methodology began.

As a documentary photographer, I had always viewed my role to experience an environment and to gather images that evoked the memory of this actual experience. This approach was proving anathema to what I was trying to accomplish by engaging in a PhD, which was to develop work that supported a central hypothesis.

As my M-phil progressed and I approached the deadline for the transfer stage to my current status as PhD student, and as I sent revision upon revision of my transfer report to my supervisor, I was urged to come up with a clear plan of action and an achievable set of goals. If I could not demonstrate that I was capable of at least this, the research board would not recommend that I progress onto a PhD – as I would clearly lack the basic skill set to complete one.

Putting aside the basic mechanical function of a camera as a recording device, photography by its very nature, is a subjective medium, which throws up a number of unique challenges when using photography as a tool to achieve some level of 'empirical' understanding.

Researchers in other areas, such as the physical sciences, are able to adopt processes that focus on producing results that can be made explicit by direct observation and duplication. Photography-led research, on the other hand, demands a methodology that embraces the implicit in order to generate results that inform practice by making unconscious mental constructs explicit: i.e. a methodology that is able to support an objective theory utilising a subjective medium.

As part of my development as a researcher, I often found it helpful to examine other methodologies contingent with the kinds of processes I was trying to develop myself, and in particular those that helped further my understanding of the semiotics of the photographic image.

One example of this was an examination of the Ethno-Methodology approach in sociological theory. Founded by the American sociologist Harold Garfinkel in the 1960's ("Studies in Ethno-methodology" 1967.) It means simply the study of the ways in which people make sense of their world. Ethno methodologists assume that social order is illusory and that society only appears to be orderly and that in reality it is chaotic ("Michel Lynch, Scientific Practice and Ordinary Action" 1997) For them social order is constructed in the minds of the individual as they experience society as a series of events which she or he must organise into a coherent pattern.

In layman's terms: other sociological perspectives assume that the social world is essentially orderly, that interaction in society is regular and systematic rather than haphazard and chaotic. Ethno methodologists assume that social order is illusory and that society only appears to be orderly and that in reality it is chaotic. For them social order is constructed in the minds of the individual as they experience society as a series of events which she or he must organise into a coherent pattern.

Garfinkel suggests that the way individuals make sense of their social world is through a psychological process called "the documentary method". (Garfinkel, H. 1967c `Common sense knowledge of social structures: The documentary method of interpretation,) A process by which people select details from social situations that seem to conform to a pattern: once this pattern has been established it is used as a framework for interpreting new facts that might arise within the situation. Garfinkel draws attention to the "indexicality"("Studies in Ethno-methodology" 1967.) of this process theorizing that people make sense of a remark, sign, or action by reference to the context in which it occurs; that is they index it to particular circumstances.

As a photographer, this theory is fascinating as it describes precisely the way in which a contemporary landscape photographer would approach their subject: by gathering data / images that are then disseminated / exhibited in very particular ways in which to create a context in which to interpret them.

There are other examples of this approach in the latter part of the 20th century, none more so than in the work of the New Topographic movement of the mid 1970's. "New Topographics" was a key exhibition that marked a turning point in the American Landscape tradition.

Opening at the International Museum of Photography at the George Eastman House, Rochester, NY in January 1975, it was made up of work from eight Amercian photographers: Robert Adams, Lewis Baltz, Frank Gohlke, Stephen Shore, Nicholas Nixon, John Schott, and Henry Wessel. The exhibition was a watershed moment in the development of a new genre of photography.

Also included in the exhibition were the prominent German couple Bernd and Hilla Becher, who had already made a name for themselves photographing industrial structures in Europe and America, exhibiting the images in series, they called "typologies", often shown in grids, under the title of "Anonymous Sculptures."

In his introduction to the catalogue, curator William Jenkins described the aesthetic of the exhibition:

"The pictures were stripped of any artistic frills and reduced to an essentially topographic state, conveying substantial amounts of visual information but eschewing entirely the aspects of beauty, emotion and opinion." ("New Topographics: Photographs of a Man-Altered Landscape" 1975)

A significant aspect of the photographers involved in the exhibition was their involvement with academia, and it is this shift from pure aesthetically or traditional documentary driven image making to a more conceptual approach to photography that marks the significance of this exhibition.

What I was able to achieve by exploring the links between Garfunkel's Ethno-Methodological approach and the New Topographical movement was a coherent strategy for the collection of practical 'data', that would allow me to develop strategies to pursue independent projects and, crucially, would enable me to 'index' (contextualise) the images within a overarching conceptual framework – thus enabling theories to be tested and conclusions drawn.

Digital Revolution

A part of my work I am also interested in the development of photography as a medium, and how this can be used in my research. I am particularly interested in the development of digital photography, and the way this has changed the way images are created, displayed, and valued.

Along with the advent of accessible digital technology, the language of photography has undergone a gradual shift. This change is not entirely new, beginning as it did in the 1990's, but it has recently gained significant momentum.

Just as websites like Wikipedia have changed the way people search for facts, photography has also become a kind of crowd-sourced media, a mechanism by which to 'consume' trends and communicate ideas in a much more free flowing and organic way that ever before.

It's not simply the technology that is of interest to my research, photography has always been about innovation, but it is the change in the context within which photographs are viewed, created, and used, that interests me.

It is not, as some might have it, the democratisation of photography – although photography is a much more accessible pastime and significantly more widespread that it was twenty years ago – there is something much more fundamental going on, more akin to the emergence of an entirely new art form.

A notorious example of this took place in 2006 when a Flickr user anonymously uploaded an image from one of the iconic photographer, Henri Cartier Bresson, claiming it as his own and inviting feedback. (http://www.flickr.com/photos/andrerabelo/70458366) Only a fraction of the Flickr users recognised the picture for what it was – and it wasn't long before there was a clamour to delete the image because of its perceived poor quality.

This incident could be interpreted on two levels. The first is a lack of knowledge of the history of photography, which, whilst not being a cardinal sin, is certainly divergent from the traditional knowledge base of a practicing photographer, the second is more fundamental. It is a disengagement from the basic tenets of photography, as if the new photography is not photography at all, but something else entirely, as divergent from photography as photography is from painting or sculpture.

Also, images have lost a lot of their intrinsic value. Just as newspapers struggle to find a way to survive the internet age, so must photographers. Copyrights are no longer respected, just as news aggregator websites draw together news stories, but don't actually write or pay for the content, blogs and other sites, link to and use photography often without permission or acknowledgment. It is as if the currency of the photographic image has changed, becoming a kind of shareware that users expect to be able to use without asking.

Another game changer is Google Street view – a remarkable portrait of every street in the UK in unprecedented detail. Websites and news aggregators no longer need to send out photographers because the images already exist. Whilst photographers are being hassled on street corners by community support officers for photographing bus stations, the Google street view car has already recorded it and put it online.

And although online resources might feel ephemeral, they are very permanent, existing in caches long after websites have been taken down: on sites such as The Way-Back-Machine, (www.archive.org) which links to over 160 million historical websites which are no longer online. Google also 'records' the internet periodically to store it for future generations – imagine if you could access Google street view of 1916 or 1945.

This change in the use of photography is relevant to my research in a number of ways. Essentially, my work is about using photography as a means of generating implicit data using a very subjective medium. In order to achieve this I must adapt a methodology that allows me to peel back the layers of history to explore the subtle vein of social engineering that runs through the chronology of new towns.

Google Street view provides the ability to plan shots ahead of time. For instance, one project I am currently working on is a Typology across all generations of new towns. To achieve this I have identified several distinctive elements of new town architecture that I believe reflect a gradual dilution of their utopian idealism.

To explore this further, I intend producing groups of images of very similar spaces in different towns that, when viewed as part of a wider project, can be used as visual shorthand to explore the changes that have taken place. This kind of project would be tremendously time consuming were it not for access to Google Street View.

Also, images linked online to the places I plan to visit offer me an opportunity to engage with an online community of individuals who chose to communicate in a predominately visual way and examine my own responses in relation to those of the 'indigenous' population.

There are many other ways, in which the development of digital photography can help my research, and by embracing this technology, as well as exploring the way in which images are 'consumed' I have been able to establish a methodology that will allow me to formulate questions using a clear set of parameters.

Loosely following the Ethno-methodological model, the following processes were used to evaluate the imagery:

- Edit and examine in detail
- Inventory 'data'
- Index images
- Look for patterns
- Form new questions
- Structure site specific projects
- Review these conclusions

Conclusion

When I began my PhD, I had a passion for the subject which remains undiminished; however, having undergone a steep learning curve, I feel I now have a much clearer and more complex understanding of the issues involved.

Pursuing a PhD can be a daunting and isolating experience, often causing one to doubt your resolve and ability to get things done, however, the learning journey required to produce research at PhD level is a rewarding and engaging one.

Each PhD is as individual as the researcher undertaking it, and the methodology developed to approach the research must also be individual. I have discussed here how I developed a way of working that has allowed me to produce tangible results, but my methodology is not perfect and is not infallible, it is a constantly changing process that must be reviewed and adapted as the work progresses.

What I hope to have achieved by shining a light on my development is to illustrate the way in which photography-led research can offer valid and robust results, which are not simply based on opinion or aesthetics, but on implicit and tangible insights.

| University of Wales, Newport | Prifysgol Cymru, Casnewydd | *Enhancing Research-Teaching Links in Higher Education*
Simon K. Haslett and Hefin Rowlands (eds)
Proceedings of the Newport NEXUS Conference
Centre for Excellence in Learning and Teaching
Special Publication, No. 3, 2010, pp. 53-58
ISBN 978-1-899274-43-7 |

The use of biodata as a predictor of student discontinuation: phase one.

Alexandra Dobson[1], Ron Fisher[2] and Mark Francis[1]

[1]Newport Business School, University of Wales, Newport, Allt-yr-yn Campus, Allt-yr-yn Avenue, Newport, NP20 5DA. Email: alexandra.dobson@newport.ac.uk
[2]Griffith Business School, Griffith University, Gold Coast campus, Qld 4222 Australia

Abstract

This paper reports on the early stages of research intended to add to the body of knowledge on why first-year students discontinue their studies prematurely. The project is cross-institutional, involving researchers from the Business School at Griffith University in Australia and from Newport Business School. In this study the use of biodata and situational judgement indices will be used to attempt to assist in identifying students at risk of withdrawal. The research is a mixed methods approach, where a qualitative stage informs the development of a quantitative stage and the focus of this paper is to consider that first qualitative stage. In both institutions this stage involves interviewing staff and students to build a list of concepts arising from the phenomena in interview transcripts, (a grounded theory approach) which will then be used to inform the quantitative use of biodata and situational judgement tests. Some 20 to 30 recorded interviews in each institution will be carried out in the first stage and the data will be analysed using both manual analysis and NVivo. Once analysis is complete, data from both institutions will be compared to highlight both similarities and differences. The goal is to develop an assessment tool that will assist in identifying students at risk of discontinuing studies prematurely. By identifying students at risk early in their university life a number of interventions can be introduced at key points to improve retention. Biodata has been shown to be an effective tool in predicting and interpreting human behaviour and has been used widely in screening for employment but is less familiar in education settings.

Introduction and Background

The stimulus for this research came from discussions around issues relating to retention generally between researchers from Newport Business School, University of Wales and the Business School, at Griffith University, Gold Coast, Australia. Clearly discontinuation of studies and the outcomes flowing from that are generally perceived to be negative for both the individual and the institution. However, some research (e.g. Parry, 2002; Charlton *et al.* 2006) takes a contrary viewpoint. Parry (2002: 17) argues that '… failing can be a positive outcome. Sometimes withdrawal, drop-out or failure to complete courses represents successful personal choices rather than failures of the student of the system". Charlton *et al.* (2006) also take the view that students leaving to take up suitable employment can be seen as a positive outcome.

Following those preliminary discussions, it was felt that an interesting and useful international co-research project could be mounted where researchers could collaborate with one another to construct an assessment tool and test it, with the overarching aim being to assist understanding in the area. The findings of the UK National Audit Office report in 2007 illustrate the scale of the problem. The report found that 'around 28,000 full-time and 87,000 part-time undergraduates who commenced their studies in 2004-05 were no longer in higher education in 2005-06. This non-continuation was estimated to result in around £30m in lost revenue, with Russell Group universities having the highest average continuation rate and the universities created since 1992 having the lowest average rate overall'.

A considerable amount of work had already been carried out at both institutions into the complex reasons why students discontinue their studies (e.g. Ramsay *et al.*, 2003; Lizzio *et al.*, 2008)**.** At Griffith, student retention is identified in its strategic and academic plans as being an area of concern that has generated a range of organizational actions. The Academic Plan (Griffith Academic Plan, 2009) in discussing student retention argues that at a University-wide level the need to 'improve capacity to identify and support students at risk' is important. The importance of improving retention is reinforced in the targets set in the academic plan and further articulated in Succeeding@Griffith (GIHE, 2009). There is no doubt that retention is important to students and the University alike, yet beyond the conventional metrics of retention commonly used to explain students' discontinuance from study there is a lack of clarity in explaining Griffith's low standing in student retention in the overall university sector in Australia.

At Griffith University, the plan to use Biodata and Situational Judgement Indices (SJI) was already underway. As a result it was felt that initially at least researchers at Griffith would take the lead by working on the Biodata measures through a process of interviews leading to development of the Situational Judgement questionnaires. The scope of the research is to investigate and develop instruments that measure, on an individual student basis, the likelihood of a student discontinuing university studies prematurely. Although the study will be aimed at first-year students it is anticipated that the measure would be applicable at any stage of a student's academic life. The

teaching question to be addressed is: *How can students at risk of prematurely discontinuing studies be identified?* The study has clear links with strategies relating to student retention more generally.

The research will develop a biographical (biodata) measure to determine the likelihood of students discontinuing first-year studies. Biodata measures are designed to measure students' non-cognitive attributes and predict multiple dimensions of university performance (Oswald *et al.*, 2004). Biodata has been shown in numerous studies to be a valid and reliable means of predicting future behaviour and performance based on questions about life and work experiences (based on the belief that future actions may frequently be predicted by past behaviours). Items such as opinions, values, beliefs, and attitudes are also considered (e.g. questions about knowledge, ethics, leadership etc). Biodata questions will be supplemented with Situational Judgment Inventory (SJI) items, both of which will invite students to select from predetermined responses. While biodata has been used extensively as a selection tool for employment and in marketing contexts (McBride *et al.*, 1997; Carraher and Carraher, 2006), it has received limited attention in educational research. While one study reports the use of biodata in higher education (Oswald *et al.*, 2004), there are no reported studies of its use in the area of student retention.

The research will advance the body of knowledge in the areas of student retention and in the use of Biodata in educational settings. It also has utility at an organisational level by providing a means for both institutions to address the issues of student retention more effectively. The purpose of the proposed research is to investigate how first-year students in the Bachelor of Business degree (at Griffith), who are likely to discontinue studies can be identified at an early stage. At NBS, the same process will be used to facilitate understanding with regard to first-year year students on the BA Business Studies.

Many issues relating to transition are well known, and a range of actions to reduce attrition has been implemented at university-level in both NBS and Griffith. However, the issue of propensity to discontinue first-year university studies *from the perspective of students themselves* has not been adequately addressed, either at the institutional level or in academic research.

Methodology

In this study a pragmatic approach is proposed (Creswell, 2000; Easterby-Smith *et al.,* 2002) using mixed methods, ensuring that a robust and sound study results through triangulation of source and method (Tashakkori and Teddlie, 1998). Firstly, a qualitative phase will collect data at each university from a range of sources including academic staff to establish a framework for conceptualising what factors lead to students discontinuing university studies prematurely. Successful students (e.g. student in Griffith Honours College) will also be interviewed in order to gain a second-order insight into success and potential failure at university (i.e. from the perspectives of the students themselves). As with all qualitative research the exact number of interviews needed to achieve saturation of concepts cannot be known *a priori* but it is estimated that up to 25 interviews will be required for each group of interviewees, a total of approximately 50 interviews. Interviews will be audio-recorded and transcribed prior to analysis, which will be undertaken using Leximancer data mining software (Smith, 2004), together with a manual process based on the constant comparison of data (Strauss and Corbin, 1990, 1998). Outputs from the qualitative phase will be used to generate and inform biodata and SJI questionnaires.

The second phase of the research will be the development and application of detailed biodata and SJI questionnaires using outputs from the qualitative phase. Questions will be developed and tested until all themes generated in the qualitative phase have been accounted for. Measurement rubrics to be used with the biodata measure will be

developed and tested. Once a questionnaire has been developed and tested it will be trialled on students enrolled in first-year business courses at each university. Data collected from questionnaires will be analysed using the measurement rubrics developed earlier. A similar approach will be adopted at Newport Business School (NBS). The number of students participating in the quantitative stage of the research will be approximately 500 at Griffith and between 50 and 100 at Newport. It should be noted that the research is at an early stage and as a result where appropriate, amendments to the methodology may take place. For instance NBS is significantly smaller than Griffith and it may be judged appropriate to interview smaller numbers of students.

Emerging Themes

Griffith University

Five interviews have been conducted at Griffith. Although in the early stages of analysis four main themes have emerged from the data:

Poor self-regulation. 'The students who are seriously thinking of deferring or dropping out of university are the ones who quite openly admit to lack of motivation' and 'and self regulation. These are the ones who are not spending a lot of time studying as much as their peers' and 'personal, social, emotional, and self-regulatory behaviours play a big part'.

Lack of career orientation. The vast majority of students, up into the 80% bracket, are first year students; they know why they came to university and for many of them it is career related' and 'I think it is a risk factor if they don't have a clear sense of purpose, I think a university has a lot of responsibility to identify those students who are lacking direction and not sure why they are here' and 'yes, I think targeted education in the first year can help students to develop that sense [of career orientation]; it is not that they either have it or they don't; for many students it is a developmental issue' and 'these were large first-year cohorts and I would talk to them about the skills they needed to develop; even if they thought something didn't seem relevant, or wasn't particularly exciting' and 'I think it is important to address some of those things [career development] head on'.

Loneliness. 'Loneliness is a major problem particularly for indigenous students' and 'not knowing anyone is a major challenge for some students' and 'finding their way around the system is a major challenge for some students'.

Lack of social skills. 'It is a combination of factors, they have got to have at the broadest level the social and cultural capital to be able to engage with university processes which are certainly alien to students, particularly those who are the first in their family to come to university' and 'so often we leave that [social capital] out of account when we are looking at skill development; we skip that step often and go straight to the basic skills of numeracy and literacy and academic literacy skills for example; and they are very important' and 'you have to look at the student life-cycle and understand where they come from and what skills they may need before they even enter the university. It is a combination of social and cultural skills as well as the academic skills that we so often emphasize; and that involves coming to terms with the ways of knowing, being and doing at a university more broadly; and how you make your way around the system and then with in a discipline or if they are doing multi-disciplinary study it makes it even more complex' and 'we expect them to come to terms with the conventions of a discipline or a range of disciplines; that is a critical set of skills that needs to make explicit rather than assumed'.

Newport Business School

At Newport, four interviews had taken place at the time of writing, all of which were amongst academic and administrative staff based in Newport Business School. Some of the emerging themes mirrored early results from Griffith. For instance *Poor Self Regulation* emerged strongly as a factor in student discontinuation but interestingly one strong theme was the difficulty which some students encounter when attempting to combine work, family life and study.

Poor Self Regulation. "Students who lack motivation are more likely to drop out, especially if they are weaker (in terms of their inherent intellectual capabilities), students to begin with. If they struggle with the some of the work, they require greater commitment. However, balanced against that factor there are students who are not so able but show high degrees of self discipline and motivation and consequently manage to complete their studies. Sometimes students do not appear to have thought carefully enough about the course they have chosen to study or cannot be persuaded to depart from a chosen path even when it becomes clear that they are struggling. For instance a student might choose a pathway that includes accountancy when they do not have the appropriate numerical skills and find it frustrating when they fail to achieve the level of success they had expected. This leads them to becoming disillusioned and then discontinuing. Sometimes this occurs even when they have been counselled not to follow a particular pathway".

Social Skills. 'You're always guaranteed that in those first couple of weeks you'll lose a couple of students because they find it difficult to make the transition when they move away from home and feel isolated. Sometimes it is surprising however because they can seem to be confident and don't obviously lack social skills but they find the move from school to University really difficult. It is not always easy to detect who will be find the transition most problematic and this makes assisting those at risk, more difficult.

In terms of working throughout the year those who have less well-developed social skills may find it more difficult but again the picture is complex. Quieter students who are highly motivated tend to stay with us, they may not appear to have such well developed social skills but as long as they form friendships, they generally do well. Again there is a strong link with motivation and judging at the outset which students possess motivation is difficult. When someone becomes isolated and particularly when they start to miss classes is often a strong indicator that they may not continue.'

Work/life balance. 'This can be really difficult for students to juggle because many of our students come from a socio/economic background that means that even when they are full-time, they need to work to support themselves as they pass through university. This can put huge strains on students and unless they are highly motivated can mean that they find the balance too difficult to maintain. In many cases, students can have additional pressures that come from having children or from responsibilities as carers. It is obviously creating an additional burden but we do have many students who manage to combine working and caring for family members and being successful academically. Factors like persistence and determination are important because those individuals who have those personality traits are likely to be able to overcome many of the obstacles.'

Discussion

It is anticipated that the research will generate academic and practical outcomes. From an academic perspective the research will advance knowledge in two ways: 1) by addressing a gap in literature concerning the application of biodata to the area of first-year retention; and 2) by advancing knowledge of first-year student retention issues. The research will also provide practical information that will assist both Griffith and Newport in understanding and managing student attrition effectively and efficiently. Application of the biodata measures early in students' university lives should identify students at risk of discontinuance of studies thus allowing strategies to be developed,

suitable support to be provided and retention to be improved.

The research will also provide opportunities for continuing studies whereby students identified at risk can be monitored throughout their university life. Identifying students at risk of discontinuing studies prematurely offers opportunities for the University to manage student retention proactively.

Conclusion

As the name of this paper implies the research is in its early stages and the authors intend to report their findings where appropriate as the research continues. The international collaborative nature of the research should yield some interesting outcomes and at this early stage there are already similarities between the findings emerging from the interviewees in both Business Schools. There are a number of reasons why the authors view this research as important. By assisting in building a picture of the characteristics that may contribute to student discontinuation the financial cost to both institutions may be lessened over time. The research while specific to Newport and Griffith will clearly have implications for other institutions and in carrying out the research the authors aim to contribute to a debate that lies at the heart of higher education. While the cost in terms of loss of revenue is important, particularly at a time when higher education is under increasing pressure it is the more subtle but pervasive effects for individuals and society that are of most interest. Leaving aside the group of students for whom discontinuation is a positive step toward some alternative pathway, it is likely that for the majority 'dropping out' will bring with it long term economic and social consequences that negatively impact on their lives.

REFERENCES

BOURNE, J. 2007. Staying the course: The retention of students in higher education. *Report by the National Audit Office,* http://web.nao.org.uk/search/search.aspx?Schema=&terms= retention.

CARRAHER, S., CARRAHER, S. 2006. Attitudes towards benefits among SME owners in Eastern Europe: a 30 month study in Belarus, Poland, and Ukraine. *Global Business and Finance Review*, 11 (1), pp. 41-48.

CHARLTON, J., BARROW, C., HORNBY-ATKINSON, P. 2006. Attempting to predict withdrawal from higher education using demographic, psychological and educational measures. *Research in Post-Compulsory Education*, 11 (1), pp. 31-47.

CRESWELL, J. 2003. *Research Design: Qualitative, Quantitative and Mixed Methods Approaches,* Thousand Oaks: Sage.

EASTERBY-SMITH, M., THORPE, R., LOWE, L. 2002. *Management Research: An Introduction.* London: Sage.

LIZZIO, A., BLUMENSTEIN, M., STEWART, A., MOODIE, G. 2008. *Evidence based retention project*. Griffith University, http://www.griffith.edu.au/office-quality-planning-statistics/improving-retention/evidence-based-retention-project

MCBRIDE, A., MENDOZA, J., CARRAHER, S. 1997. Development of a biodata index to measure service-orientation. *Psychological Reports*, 81, pp.1395-407.

NICKLES, B. 1994. The nature of biodata, in Stokes, G.S., Mumford, M.D., Owens, W.A. (Eds), *Biodata Handbook: Theory, Research, and Use of Biographical Information in Selection and Performance Prediction*, Consulting Psychologists Press, Palo Alto, CA, pp.1-16.

OSWALD, F., SCHMITT, N., KIM, B., RAMSAY, L., GILLESPIE, M. 2004. Developing a biodata measure and situational judgment inventory as predictors of college student performance, *Journal of Applied Psychology*, 89, pp.187-207.

PARRY, G. 2002. A short history of failure. In Peelo, M and Wareham, T (eds), *Failing Students in Higher Education*, Buckinghamshire: Open University Press, pp. 15-28.

RAMSAY.S. ELPHINSONE, L. VIVECKANANDA,K. 2003. *Griffith University Student Retention Project,* Griffith University. http://www.griffith.edu.au/cms-secure/learning-teaching/ retention.pdf

SMITH, A. 2004. *Leximancer Manual (ver 2.0)*, [PDF File installed with Leximancer program].

STRAUSS, A., CORBIN, J. 1990. *Basics of Qualitative Research: Grounded theory procedures and techniques.* Newbury Park, Sage.

STRAUSS, A., CORBIN, J. 1998. *Basics of Qualitative Research: Techniques and procedures for developing grounded theory.* Thousand Oaks: Sage.

TASHAKKORI, A., TEDDLIE, C. 1998. *Mixed Methodology: Combining Qualitative and Quantitative Approaches*. Thousand Oaks: Sage.

WEST, J., KARAS, M. 1999. Biodata: Meeting clients needs for a better way of recruiting entry-level staff. *International Journal of Selection and Assessment*, 7 (2), pp.

YORKE, M., LONGDEN, B. 2008. The first-year experience of higher education in the UK. *Final Report,* York: The Higher Education Academy, http://www.heacademy.ac.uk/assets/York/documents/resources/publications/FYEFinalReport.pdf

University of Wales, Newport

Prifysgol Cymru, Casnewydd

Enhancing Research-Teaching Links in Higher Education
Simon K. Haslett and Hefin Rowlands (eds)
Proceedings of the Newport NEXUS Conference
Centre for Excellence in Learning and Teaching
Special Publication, No. 3, 2010, pp. 59-69
ISBN 978-1-899274-43-7

Future is due: reflecting on local and global practice to discover effective sustainability.

Tatiana Diniz and Alison Glover

Centre for Excellence in Learning and Teaching, University of Wales, Newport, Lodge Road, Caerleon, South Wales, NP18 3QT. Email: tatiana.diniz@newport.ac.uk; alison.glover@newport.ac.uk

Abstract

Education for Sustainable Development and Global Citizenship (ESDGC) demands an interdisciplinary approach and is calling for attention in all disciplines, from the social sciences to engineering. It should act as a common room where expertise can be shared in order to identify future practice that is beyond the specific knowledge within each field. Furthermore, its relevance has been acknowledged by both government and funding agencies and it already figures as a key element of concern for shaping future policies within higher education. This paper explores the concept of sustainability and its boundaries, drawing on current practice led by universities in different contexts, the United Kingdom and Latin America. Recent research findings from Brazil and Wales will be presented via a virtual journey illustrating how universities are approaching sustainability in different global contexts. This aims to demonstrate that sustainability can mean different things and that there are various ways of engaging with students and staff. This work is part of an empowerment workshop which includes the use of images, allowing participants to explore personal interpretations of sustainability and determine the importance and relevance of presented concepts to their department and institution. The intention being for participants to decide on the possible paths their department and institution could engage in towards sustainability by reflecting on priorities for effective action within their institution.

Introduction

This paper focuses on approaches to Education for Sustainable Development and Global Citizenship (ESDGC) which have been applied in higher education institutions in Brazil and Wales. Currently the United Nations Decade of Education for Sustainable Development (2005-2014) is underway and endeavours to integrate sustainable development into all education sectors. The case studies presented here form part of a workshop, aimed at raising awareness of practices already underway in higher education. The intention is also to encourage critical thinking regarding understanding and interpretation of the terms 'sustainability' and 'Education for Sustainable Development and Global Citizenship'.

Loeber et al. (2007) define sustainable development as 'an essentially *contestable* concept, in the sense that no authoritative, universally valid definition can be formulated. There is no way of determining what is 'really sustainable' other than through processes of collective and contextual deliberation and mutual learning' (Loeber et al. 2007, p. 84). Also according to these authors, the concept claims '*normatively*, to offer desirable directions for action. Hence, the learning

59

processes implied in the first characteristics are more than mere 'joint fact finding' exercises, and involve processes of value judgement. From both characteristics, it follows that the sustainable development concepts need to be elaborated in an 'action-oriented' way, in which a balance is found between what is deemed desirable and what may be made feasible, given a particular context.' (Loeber et al. 2007, p. 84)

Higher education has been singled out as producing people who contribute to unsustainable practices (Orr, 1994; Martin and Jucker, 2003; Blewitt, 2004b). It is time for higher education to lead by example in engaging completely with its 'responsibility to be a place where new answers can be sought, choices widened and thinking encouraged' (Blewitt, 2004a, p. 32). However, it has been suggested that a major problem facing higher education is the limitation presented when trying to create a sustainable university in an unsustainable society (Clugston, 2004, p. x). Nevertheless Clugston continues by suggesting the way forward needs to involve not only 'deep reflection on the nature of the educational transformation' but 'practical examples of how institutions in diverse cultural settings have successfully reoriented their teaching and research, outreach and operations to embody their own forms of sustainability' (Clugston, 2004, p. x).

These aspects of sustainable development should be embedded in any discussion about the case studies presented by this paper, as none of them should be accepted as ideal, but as an effort towards action within a specific context and, therefore, as inspiration for diverse action-oriented efforts. To begin with overviews of the higher education sectors in Brazil and Wales are presented, including key elements of the ESDGC journey for the countries. This is followed by the practical examples from the diverse cultures of Brazilian and Welsh higher education. By studying existing action individuals and institutions may be assisted in reorienting and innovating activities both within the campus and the curriculum, which

in turn will be valuable as they drive for effective sustainability.

Higher Education in Brazil

Brazil is a country with an estimated population of 183.9 million (IBGE, Brazilian Institute for Geography and Statistics, 2009). Politically, it is divided into 27 Estates spread over five geographic regions; north, northeast, southeast, central-west and south. There are 12 main urban centres, listed by relevance: São Paulo, Rio de Janeiro, Brasília, Manaus, Belém, Fortaleza, Recife, Salvador, Belo Horizonte, Curitiba, Porto Alegre and Goiânia (IBGE, 2007).

Historically, Brazil was a Portuguese colony between 1500 and 1822, mostly exporting crops and importing industrialised products. Higher education provision started by the end of this period, and it was initially designed for the needs of the local white European elite, who acted as a small group of decision-makers over a mixed, black slave and indigenous majority. In 1808, army and navy institutes for higher education were created, followed by the first courses of medicine, engineering, economy, chemistry, agriculture and law (Aranha, 2003, p.153-154).

According to recent data, a total of 2,252 institutions provide for higher education in Brazil, 236 public and 2,016 private. They are defined as universities, university centres and faculties. Public provision is funded by government at national (*federal*), estate (*estadual*) or city (*municipal*) levels. Over 5 million people are enrolled in higher education in Brazil, which represents less than a quarter of those of educational age in the country (MEC/INEP, 2009).

The origins of ESDGC in Brazil are deeply linked to the evolution of Environmental Education (EE) in the country. EE was introduced as a complementary tool to support the implementation of a national environmental policy. Therefore, it was placed on the government's agenda in 1988, when the new Brazilian constitution formally recognized the right for all Brazilian citizens to receive Environmental Education. This emphasised a commitment towards "promoting EE at all educational levels and encouraging public awareness regarding environmental protection" (SECAD/MEC, 2007, p.19).

To a certain extent, a lack of reflection on the role to be played by higher education institutions has been one of the features of the evolution of Brazilian EE. Most of the legislation and debates focused on compulsory education. In 2006, however, a study analysed current practice within 22 higher education institutions (from which 14 were public and eight, private) situated in 11 different Estates. The aim was to obtain general information regarding actions, projects and internal bodies/structures related to EE as well as identifying difficulties, and catalysts for the implementation of EE in the studied universities (SECAD/MEC, 2007, p. 24). The results of MEC's study illustrated that the bulk of EE practice carried out by Brazilian higher education was not initiated by official institutional policies but more often by spontaneous drives towards social responsibility. Figure 1 provides a timeline of ESD in Brazil.

Timeline: the Brazilian journey towards ESD

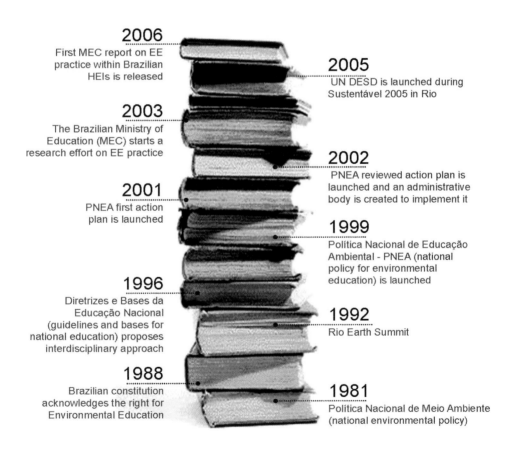

2006
First MEC report on EE practice within Brazilian HEIs is released

2005
UN DESD is launched during Sustentável 2005 in Rio

2003
The Brazilian Ministry of Education (MEC) starts a research effort on EE practice

2002
PNEA reviewed action plan is launched and an administrative body is created to implement it

2001
PNEA first action plan is launched

1999
Política Nacional de Educação Ambiental - PNEA (national policy for environmental education) is launched

1996
Diretrizes e Bases da Educação Nacional (guidelines and bases for national education) proposes interdisciplinary approach

1992
Rio Earth Summit

1988
Brazilian constitution acknowledges the right for Environmental Education

1981
Política Nacional de Meio Ambiente (national environmental policy)

Figure 1. The Brazilian journey towards ESD.

This idea of informality as an action-driver within Brazilian institutions may contribute to a better understanding of how projects within higher education can often be triggered by elements other than well-structured policies. Indeed, different university-led 'hands-on' approaches related to ESD have been described in the recent literature, as presented in the next section of this paper, even though the Brazilian governmental approach around ESD is still budding. The next section presents a sample of sustainability projects supported or led by higher education in Brazil. Figure 2 illustrates their location.

Brazilian Case Studies

Solar Power for Low Income Population

In the city of Sao Paulo, in the southeast of Brazil, SoSol (*Sociedade do Sol*, the Sun Society) is the name of a social enterprise initiative incubated by Cietec (the University of Sao Paulo's technological business incubator). It is an independent initiative supported as a "resident project", which means having a low cost equipped office and relying on technical support from the university enterprise incubator. SoSol delivers short training programmes on renewable energy. Its most popular course teaches how to make a low cost solar water heater system to supply home showers and has been attracting brick layers to post graduate students from different fields, including construction industry managers and government housing officers (SoSol, 2009).

Fees are charged for the training, they are not expensive and a small number of bursaries are offered to colleagues from Cietec. Parallel to the courses, SoSol acts as an independent research lab for renewable energy, concentrating efforts on developing new applications for solar water heating, such as more complex models to be installed in hotels, hospitals and social housing building projects. The technology is intentionally not registered and its use is free of charges and patents. The scheme generates a network of learners and facilitators who exchange information amongst themselves and contribute to innovation within the project. The innovation has spread worldwide, with self-made tutors taught in Brazil now applying skills in countries such as Mexico, India and Germany, always as a "social technology" (SoSol, 2009).

Other programmes addressing wind power, photovoltaic energy, rainwater collecting systems and environmental education to schools can be delivered by SoSol depending on demand. Furthermore, donations are collected to build up small models of the solar water heater, which are donated to local schools, with a short training for the teachers. In schools, the models are applied to help students learn different disciplines, from science to mathematics (SoSol, 2009).

Recycling and Income Generation

In the central-west, a partnership between the Universidade Católica de Goiás (Catholic University of Goiás) and Dom Fernando Institute (IDF), a local charity, implemented a university extension course that empowered members of 31 poor families living by the Meia Ponte River to run a waste recycling cooperative named Cooprec. The initiative provided environmental education and income generation, and the average amount of waste collected and recycled by the cooperative has been approximately 50,000 kilos per month (Borges and Teixeira, 2005). Five years after the initial training with the community, Cooprec is a national reference on recycling and produces innovative products such as eco-friendly roof material made from recycled card.

Nevertheless, in an analysis of the extension programme led by the Catholic University of Goias and the IDF charity, Borges and Teixeira (2005, p. 25) recognized that although being trained to work in recycling, the members of Cooprec failed to perceive that people are responsible for the waste they produce, and do not make the link between waste, consumption and lifestyle. The priority appeared to be the urgent need for income generation. Therefore, even though the community was receiving training, delivered by higher education, to join an up-to-date green activity, community participants were not always educated to create meaning to their own sustainability experience.

Case studies in different Brazilian regions

1. Monções – Looking after Biodiversity
UFMA - staff and students from the Biological Science Department are involved in community education, community training and actions towards environmental protection.

2. São Paulo – Solar Power for Low Income Population
Cietec/USP - a social enterprise delivers short training programmes on renewable energy, teaching how to make low cost solar water heaters to supply home showers.

3. Goiânia – Recycling and Income Generation
UCG - an extension course empowered members of 31 poor families living by the Meia Ponte River to run a waste recycling cooperative.

4. Altamira - Sustainable Honey
UFPA - beekeepers living along the Transamazônica road area, in the Amazon forest learn sustainable techniques of honey production.

5. Viçosa - E-learning for Green Enterprise
Free e-learning modules include green enterprise skills, as how to make eco-friendly soap by recycling used cooking oil

6. Porto Alegre - Green Bricks
FURG - community training in how to make bricks for construction, using sustainable material and techniques

Figure 2. Location of Brazilian case studies.

63

Looking after Biodiversity

In the northeast of Brazil, a university-based enterprise company *(empresa-junior)* called *Mutual* engages staff and students from the Biological Science Department of the Federal University of Maranhão (UFMA), in community education, community training and actions towards environmental protection. Current projects include developing a community-based ecotourism system in Moncoes, a region that holds a particularly rich biodiversity, and the efforts are to locally ensure both social and environmental sustainability (Mutual, 2009).

Green Bricks and Sustainable Honey

In the south, one of the extension courses offered by the Federal University of Rio Grande (FURG) in 2009 provided community training in how to make bricks for construction, using sustainable materials and techniques, in order to generate income and local jobs and allow better and greener popular housing (FURG, 2009).

In the north, an extension project of the Altamira's campus of the Federal University of Pará (UFPA) provides training for the beekeepers living along the Transamazônica road area, in the Amazon forest, teaching them sustainable techniques of honey production (UFPA, 2009).

E-learning: making soap with cooking oil

Overcoming geographical barriers to community education, the University of Viçosa (UFV) created a series of free e-learning modules developed by its researchers to be offered online to small/medium entrepreneurs as its main audience, although open to anyone interested. In July 2009, Dr Marisa Alvez Nogueira Diaz, a senior lecturer in Chemistry at UFV, launched an online course that applied some of her scientific discoveries in a method that teaches how to make eco-friendly soap by recycling used cooking oil (UFV/Portal do Produtor, 2009).

Higher Education in Wales

Wales is a nation with a population of 2.98 million (Welsh Assembly Government, 2010). The main urban centres are Cardiff, Newport and Swansea in the South of the country, and Wrexham in the North. Twelve higher education institutions employ more than 6,800 staff and educate over 120,000 full and part time students from Wales and further afield. The sector currently receives more than £356 million of funding from the Welsh Assembly Government, which is allocated to institutions via the Higher Education Funding Council for Wales. The nation is governed by the United Kingdom Government with some devolution of powers to the Welsh Assembly Government, established in 1999.

Section 79 of the Government of Wales Act 2006 Chapter 32, refers specifically to the functions of the Welsh Assembly Government promoting sustainable development. Section 60 of the Government of Wales Act states;
The Welsh Ministers may do anything which they consider appropriate to achieve any one or more of the following objectives
(a) the promotion or improvement of the economic well-being of Wales,
(b) the promotion or improvement of the social well-being of Wales, and
(c) the promotion or improvement of the environmental well-being of Wales.
(Office of Public Sector Information, 2006, p.35).

The Welsh Assembly Government is responsible for Education and training policies across the nation. It is also required to implement initiatives directly from the United Kingdom Government; relevant to this discussion is the adoption of the United Kingdom's shared framework for sustainable development (2005) quoted in Welsh Assembly documentation (Welsh Assembly Government, 2006, p. 30, 2008, p. 53, 2009, p. 51). However, the development and implementation of prioritising sustainable development within Wales is very much driven by the Welsh Assembly Government.

Timeline: some important dates for Welsh ESDGC

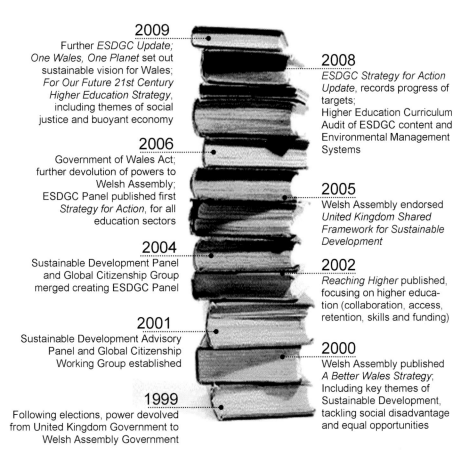

2009
Further *ESDGC Update;*
One Wales, One Planet set out
sustainable vision for Wales;
For Our Future 21st Century
Higher Education Strategy,
including themes of social
justice and buoyant economy

2008
ESDGC Strategy for Action
Update, records progress of
targets;
Higher Education Curriculum
Audit of ESDGC content and
Environmental Management
Systems

2006
Government of Wales Act;
further devolution of powers to
Welsh Assembly;
ESDGC Panel published first
Strategy for Action, for all
education sectors

2005
Welsh Assembly endorsed
United Kingdom Shared
Framework for Sustainable
Development

2004
Sustainable Development Panel
and Global Citizenship Group
merged creating ESDGC Panel

2002
Reaching Higher published,
focusing on higher educa-
tion (collaboration, access,
retention, skills and funding)

2001
Sustainable Development Advisory
Panel and Global Citizenship
Working Group established

2000
Welsh Assembly published
A Better Wales Strategy;
Including key themes of
Sustainable Development,
tackling social disadvantage
and equal opportunities

1999
Following elections, power devolved
from United Kingdom Government to
Welsh Assembly Government

Figure 3. Key dates for ESDGC in Wales.

Since the establishment of a National Curriculum for schools in 1988, sustainable development and global citizenship has been included in the school sector curriculum and ESDGC now forms part of the inspection framework in Wales. Higher education is allowed autonomy of its curriculum, and coverage of ESDGC is currently not mandatory within the sector. However, in 2008 the Welsh Assembly Government funded audits of ESDGC curriculum content in higher education and feedback concerning Environmental Management Systems. Such actions reflect some commitment to ESDGC and this is also evident in the succession of *ESDGC Strategies for Action* (Welsh Assembly Government, 2006, 2008 and 2009). Figure 3 illustrates key dates for Wales and ESDGC and Figure 4 identifies the location of the case studies, presented and discussed during the workshop.

Welsh Case Studies

PONT Community to Community

In 2005 a partnership between the South Wales town of Pontypridd and the Mbale region of Uganda was formalised. Initially partnership links were established between medical organisations, schools and churches. More recently staff volunteers from the University of Glamorgan have formed the Glamorgan PONT Board (PONT – Partnership Overseas Networking Trust). Many projects have been undertaken, with the aim being to empower people to develop and realise ideas (PONT – Mbale, 2010). Key Non-Governmental Organisations in Uganda work with the PONT partnership in implementing new initiatives. Some of the United Nations Millennium Goals, such as better sanitation and secure tenure, provide underlying targets for the projects in Uganda (PONT – Mbale, 2010).

Case studies in Wales

1. University of Glamorgan: Community Links
Staff and students engage in linking their community with a region of Uganda; fundraising and providing assistance for development projects in Uganda.

2. Glyndŵr University: Energy Monitoring
Students use energy monitoring data in their studies; critically assessing areas of the campus and making recommendations for improvements.

3. University of Wales, Newport: Production of Biodiesel
Waste vegetable oil is processed on site into biodiesel and used in university vehicles on campus and on the public highway.

4. Swansea University and Swansea Metropolitan University: Living Sustainably Module
Collaboration between two institutions to deliver a 'Living Sustainably' module to students and staff.

Figure 4. Location of Welsh case studies.

Since the University has become involved with the initiative many staff and students have visited the Mbale region of Uganda and participated in projects, which include among many others; a payroll-giving scheme to PONT with staff deciding what projects to spend funds on; working in schools (teaching mathematics or as classroom assistants); testing water quality to assist engineers providing clean water supplies for local communities and a recently established research and development centre, at the University of Glamorgan, focusing on connecting communities. All visits to Uganda are self-funded, students organise fundraising events to support their trips, with several making return visits and some aiming to undertake longer work placements with future development projects. March 2010 saw the University PONT team, alongside other partners, awarded two 'United Nations Gold Star' Awards under 'livelihoods' and the 'environment' categories.

Energy Monitoring by Students

In 2008 the Higher Education Funding Council for Wales (HEFCW) allocated funds of £3.8million to permit the installation of integrated systems of sub metering to enable monitoring and targeting of 90% of energy and water consumption within Welsh Higher Education Institutions (HEFCW, 2007). Glyndŵr University, Wrexham received approximately £185,000 to fund the installation of hardware and energy improvements.

Students studying the 'Building Appraisal and Maintenance' module originate from several degree pathways and work groups are created ensuring a mix of students from different degree courses, during their final year. The piece of coursework utilising the monitoring data forms one of three pieces for this module, providing 30% of the module assessment. Approximately 15 – 20 students choose to take the module.

The aim of the coursework is to produce a critical appraisal of the energy consumption for a selected area of the campus. The reports receive a group assessment resulting from the final written report. The process includes monthly presentations to the other groups and a final presentation by each group with the Estates Department also present. The first cohort of students to critically appraise the real situation at Glyndwr regarding energy consumption took place in 2009. Their reports made recommendations, some of which Estates have addressed and some which have formed the basis for the appraisals by the next cohort of students.

Student feedback from module evaluation has been positive for example; 'nice to do a practical project of real benefit', with ex-students commenting 'it got me the job', 'at interview I was the only university candidate with real practical knowledge' (Jones, 2010). Much interest has been generated across the institution as a result of the students' work and other disciplines, for example Business and Information Technology, are incorporating the energy monitoring data into their courses, with other disciplines exploring the potential of using the information in the future.

Processing and use of biodiesel

Since 2007 the University of Wales, Newport, has processed and used biodiesel, utilising waste cooking oil from its catering facilities. A biodiesel processor and related equipment was purchased for £7500. The biodiesel is used in grounds maintenance vehicles, on campus, and in the post bus, which travels on the public highway between two campuses.

Between February 2007 and September 2009 the biodiesel project recycled 5200 litres of waste vegetable oil potentially saving 78% in carbon dioxide emissions compared to petroleum diesel (Pahl, 2008), with fewer sulphates, less smoke and particulate matter emitted (Bozbas, 2008). Manufacturing the fuel on site has meant cost savings of approximately 75% compared to purchasing fossil fuels. It has been calculated that all initial costs have been recovered in the first three years of the initiative. Capital is being reinvested into the project aiming to continually improve the process and quality of fuel. The project was recognised in the Envirowise 2010 Public Sector Waste and Sustainability Awards winning the Innovation Award category.

Living Sustainably Module

Since 2004 Swansea Metropolitan University and Swansea University have worked in collaboration to deliver a module originally entitled 'Application of Sustainable Development Principles', more recently altered to 'Living Sustainably'. Delivery of the module takes place during the day time or evening at either institution, this means students from the two institutions work together. A Welsh Assembly grant for Education for Sustainable Development and Global Citizenship projects was used initially to market the module extensively. The module is 100% coursework and aims 'to give students an appreciation of sustainability in practice and, to enable them to apply sustainability to themselves; in their own study area, lives, job roles, families, local communities or organisations.' (May, 2006)

A total of 25 students enrolled for 2004-5 and numbers have gradually increased over following years. The module is optional resulting in a mixture of part-time and full-time students, from different disciplines studying it. Members of staff have also enrolled and the module is recognised within the staff development programme. The module was recognised with a Global Learning Award in 2007, presented by Cyfanfyd, an organisation funded by the Department for International Development.

Summary

The intention of this collation of case study material is to encourage the discussion of real possibilities to the approach of ESDGC within higher education. A broad spectrum of examples has been considered; including those which target greening the university campus, embedding sustainability within the curricula and developing community links. The examples have involved collaboration between higher education institutions and across discipline areas as well as outreach initiatives, which has been the predominant approach in Latin America. It is anticipated that a developing appreciation of interpretations of sustainability continues to emerge as individuals assimilate and reflect on the issues raised.

Acknowledgements

We are grateful to Girafa Nao Fala Design Grafico (Sao Paulo, Brazil) for designing the images that illustrate the Brazilian data.
Augustin T. Woelz, Sociedade do Sol coordinator;
CIETEC/USP (University of Sao Paulo Technological Business Incubator); TEIA-USP (University of Sao Paulo Environment and Education Lab);
NEF PUC-SP (Catholic University of Sao Paulo Centre of Studies for the Future) for supporting fieldwork in Brazil.
Professor David Jenkins (University of Glamorgan);
Derek Jones, (Glyndwr University, Wrexham);
Matthew Bellamy, (University of Wales, Newport); and
Elizabeth May, (Swansea Metropolitan University) for their assistance in compiling the data for these case studies.

REFERENCES

AUDITOR GENERAL FOR WALES, 2005. *Energy and Water Management in the Higher Education Sector in Wales*. Cardiff: National Audit Office Wales.

ARANHA, M.L.A.A. 2003. *História da Educação,* Sao Paulo: Editora Moderna.

BLEWITT, J. 2004a. Sustainability and Lifelong Learning. In: BLEWITT, J. and CULLINGFORD, C. eds. *The Sustainability Curriculum – The Challenge for Higher Education*, London: Earthscan. pp. 24 – 42.

BLEWITT, J. 2004b. Introduction. In: BLEWITT, J. and CULLINGFORD, C. eds. *The Sustainability*

Curriculum – The Challenge for Higher Education, London: Earthscan. pp. 1 – 9.

BORGES, A.L.G., and TEIXEIRA, L.S.C (2005). *Reciclagem de lixo e cooperativa popular - construindo uma metodologia de trabalho.* Anais do IIII Encontro Internacional de Economia Solidária: Desenvolvimento Local, Trabalho e Autonomia.

BOZBAS, K. 2008. Biodiesel as an alternative motor fuel: Production and policies in the European Union. *Renewable and Sustainable Energy Reviews.* 12, (2), pp.542 – 552.

CLUGSTON, R. 2004. Foreword. In: CORCORAN,P. and WALS, A. eds. *Higher Education and the Challenges of Sustainability Problematics, Promise and Practice,* Netherlands: Kluwer Academic Publishers. pp. ix – xii.

HEFCW, 2007. *Newsletter, Issue Number 1, May 2007.* Available at: http://www.hefcw.ac.uk/documents/news/newsletter/HEFCW%20Newsletter%20No%201%20-%20May%202007.pdf (16 April 2019).

IBGE, Brazilian Institute for Geography and Statistics, 2009).

JONES, D. 2010. (21 April 2010). *Energy Monitoring Questions.* [E-mail]. E-mail to A Glover (21 April 2010).

LOEBER, B.M., GRIN, J., and LEEUWIS, C, 2007. The Practical Value of Theory. In: WALS, A.E.J: Social Learning Towards a Sustainable World. Principles, Perspectives and Praxis. The Netherlands: Wageningen Academic Publishers.

MARTIN, S. and JUCKER, R. 2003. Educating Earth-Literate Leaders. Keynote at *International Association of Universities Prague Conference, Education for a Sustainable Future.* Available at http://www.unesco.org/iau/sd/pdf/Jucker-Martins.pdf (7 Feb 2010).

MAY, E. 2006. (19 April 2010). *Summative Module Report.* [E-mail]. E-mail to A Glover (19 April 2010).

MEC/INEP (BRAZILIAN MINISTRY OF EDUCATION and ANÍSIO TEIXEIRA NATIONAL INSTITUTE FOR EDUCATIONAL RESEARCH), 2009. *Resumo Técnico: Censo da Educação Superior (Dados Preliminares).* Brasília-DF.

MUTUAL, 2009 *Projetos.* Available at: http://ejmutual.com.br/empresa/projetos (9 September 2009).

OFFICE OF PUBLIC SECTOR INFORMATION, 2006. *Government of Wales Act 2006 Chapter 32,* http://www.opsi.gov.uk/acts/acts2006/ukpga_20060032_en_1 (5 Jan 2010).

ORR, D. 1994. *Earth in Mind, On Education and the Human Prospect.* Washington: Island Press.

PONT – Mbale, 2010. *Aims.* http://pont-mbale.org.uk/main/en/overview/aims (19 April 2010).

PAHL, G. 2008. *Biodiesel: Growing a New Energy Economy.* USA: Chelsea Green Publishing Company.

SECRETARIA EXECUTIVA DE COORDENAÇÃO GERAL DE EDUCAÇÃO AMBIENTAL/MINISTÉRIO DA EDUCAÇÃO/ (SECAD/MEC) (not dated). *Educação ambiental e sustentabilidade: formação para a cidadania* [Online] http://portal.mec.gov.br/secad/arquivos/pdf/coea/educsust.pdf (23 June 2009).

SOSOL, 2009. *ASBC: Aquecedor Solar de Baixo Custo.* Available at: http://www.sosol.org.br (7 March 2010).

UFPA, 2009. Universidade Federal do Pará. Available at: http://www3.ufpa.br/multicampi/images/LINK/PROJETOS%20DE%20EXTEN%C7%C3O%20DO%20CAMPUS%20DE%20SANTAR%C9M.pdf (7 March 2010).

FURG, 2009. Universidade federal do Rio Grande. Available at: http://www.furg.br/supext (12 September 2009).

UFV/PORTAL DO PRODUTOR (2009) Universidade Federal de Viçosa. Available at: https://www2.cead.ufv.br/espacoProdutor/scripts/verCurso.php (7 March 2010).

WELSH ASSEMBLY GOVERNMENT, 2006. *Education for Sustainable Development and Global Citizenship – A Strategy for Action.* DELLS Information Document No: 017 -06.

WELSH ASSEMBLY GOVERNMENT, 2008. *Education for Sustainable Development and Global Citizenship – A Strategy for Action.* Information Document No: 055/2008.

WELSH ASSEMBLY GOVERNMENT, 2009. *Education for Sustainable Development and Global Citizenship – A Strategy for Action.* Information Document No: 077/2009.

WELSH ASSEMBLY GOVERNMENT, 2010. *Wales's Population 2009.* http://wales.gov.uk/topics/statistics/headlines/pop2009/hdw200903262/?skip=1&lang=en (24 March 2010).

University of Wales, Newport

Prifysgol Cymru, Casnewydd

Enhancing Research-Teaching Links in Higher Education
Simon K. Haslett and Hefin Rowlands (eds)
Proceedings of the Newport NEXUS Conference
Centre for Excellence in Learning and Teaching
Special Publication, No. 3, 2010, pp. 70-82
ISBN 978-1-899274-43-7

Linking geohazard research programmes with the development of teaching and learning exercises: an example of using urban landslides in the South Wales coalfield.

Peter John Brabham and Alessia Taboga

School of Earth and Ocean Sciences, Cardiff University, Cardiff, CF10 3YE, United Kingdom.
Email: Brabham@cardiff.ac.uk

Abstract

The South Wales coalfield has one of the highest densities of inland landslides in the UK. Commonly landslides occur on the densely populated valley sides, especially during a period of heavy rainfall, which then threaten housing or disrupt the urban infrastructure. In October 1966, South Wales was the location of the UK's greatest landslide disaster at Aberfan resulting in 144 fatalities. Over the post-Aberfan period, millions of pounds have been spent remediating colliery tip and natural landslide sites throughout the valleys. Important landslide information from these ground engineering projects has now been made available in a series of publications by the National Museum of Wales revealing the multi-factor nature of these landslides. Between 2006–2010, the authors have been undertaking an EPSRC industrially sponsored PhD research programme into the development of new techniques in the photogrammetric and geophysical mapping of selected urban landslides. A spin-off from the research study is that new teaching and learning exercises at both BSc and Masters' level have been developed in parallel to train Cardiff University students in quantitative geohazard analysis. A four-stage education programme is described, combining a conventional lecture, computer-based geographical information systems (GIS) studies, a one-day landslide fieldcourse and a follow-up landslide site investigation programme. The fieldcourse has strategically-staged visits, initially observing colliery tip failure sites at Cilfynydd and Aberfan in the Taff valley, followed by a tour down the Rhondda Fawr Valley studying many mass movement sites. These sites include the A4061 Rhigos road, plus the Blaencwm, Pentre and Mynydd yr Eglwys landslides. The active 1998 landslide at Mynydd yr Eglwys has then been further utilised for the development of new quantitative field-training exercises linking symbiotically with the PhD research programme.

Introduction

The School of Earth and Ocean Sciences at Cardiff University has a diverse portfolio of staff, with wide-ranging research interests. One of the research groups works on applied geo-environmental problems and staff within this research group are responsible for teaching two postgraduate taught Masters' level courses in Applied Environmental Geology and Environmental Hydrogeology. At undergraduate level the School offers four subject pathways: Geology, Exploration Geology, Marine Geography and Environmental Geoscience (Brabham, 2009b). The subject of geohazards is taught across all four pathways at all academic levels. In the UK, global geohazards such as earthquakes, volcanic eruptions, tsunamis and landslides are popular subjects with students at all academic levels. However, because the UK is not located at a Plate Tectonic Boundary, geohazards do not actually normally impinge directly on the UK population's day to day lives. Unusually, in April 2010, the ash cloud from the Icelandic Eyjafjallajökull volcanic eruption grounded all UK air traffic for six days making national front page news. Probably for the first time in the modern era a geohazard has had a major UK countrywide impact.

The first author of this paper has over two decades of experience teaching geohazards as a conventional undergraduate classroom module. It is certainly true that it is easier today to accumulate a vast number of geohazard teaching and learning resources than it has ever been. Earthquakes and volcanoes are extensively described in glossy North American introductory geoscience text books and there are a huge number of geohazard resources available via the internet (e.g. Marshak, 2007). BBC documentary programmes such as Horizon also regularly cover earthquake, tsunami and volcanic hazards. Global case studies such as the San Andreas fault, the 2004 Indian Ocean tsunami or the Montserrat volcanic event can be developed relatively easily. No doubt the Icelandic Eyjafjallajökull volcano event will produce many more case studies in future years for UK students to study.

Given the abundant availability of resource material, it is relatively easy to teach geohazards qualitatively. This in itself, if well taught, can engender an early enthusiasm for Earth studies in schoolchildren at both primary and secondary levels. The question is how can teachers approach the subject of geohazards in a more quantitative manner? One solution is to run expensive overseas fieldcourses for undergraduates and A-Level geography students, with Iceland, Mount Etna, Vesuvius or the French Alps being popular destinations (Giles *et al.*, 2008). Such fieldcourses are expensive (£500-£1000 per head) but are rewarding in that they provide students with an "experience" just not available in the UK (Giles *et al.*, 2008). In this modern era of virtual reality fieldcourses and Google Earth one must question the economic and educational sense in taking a party of students thousands of miles to give a "lecture in the field" (Giles *et al.*, 2008). If one wants to incorporate quantitative geohazard field measurements into overseas fieldcourses, then this can be logistically difficult because of the scale of the site, local politics and the requirement to take all surveying equipment with you. The solution may be then to buy into overseas educational packages run by professional companies offering a hands-on programme of student field-based learning tasks.

If we are looking at developing an educationally rigorous, but more economic UK geohazard experience then landslides are probably the best geohazard subject to concentrate studies in the UK. Popular landslide subject areas are active coastal landslides where coastal erosion constantly causes landsliding in softer geological rocks. The Dorset coast (Lyme Regis to Charmouth), Isle of Wight (Ventnor), North Yorkshire (Scarborough) or North Wales (Llyn) are popular sites to study (Giles *et al.*, 2008).

This paper describes a four-stage programme of integrated teaching and learning steps leading to a quantitative research study of an active urban landslide in the South Wales valleys. The full educational programme described is followed by students enrolled on the vocational MSc degree in Applied Environmental Geology (Brabham, 2009b), but the programme could be adapted for use at academic level 6. The geomorphological mapping component has also been adapted for basic field skills training for level 5 BSc Environmental Geoscience students. These teaching and learning exercises have been developed alongside a parallel EPSRC-funded landslide PhD research programme undertaken by the second author (Taboga, 2010). This PhD research programme has supplied detailed geomorphological base maps, topographic maps, ground surveying stations, borehole measurements, plus a library of historical data on ground movement and rainfall for the educational programme. Additional data has been supplied by other agencies such as Halcrow Ltd and Rhondda Cynon Taff Council.

Landslides in the South Wales valleys

The South Wales Coalfield has one of the highest concentrations of landslides in the United Kingdom (Conway *et al.*, 1980) and was also the location of the worst landslide disaster in the UK at Aberfan (McLean and Johnes, 2000). The Aberfan colliery tip failure of 21st October 1966 resulted in 144 fatalities, with 116 children killed as a result of colliery spoil engulfing the village school (Penman, 2000). As a result of the Aberfan disaster and the subsequent post 1985 demise of the South Wales deep coal mining industry, most colliery tips in South Wales have now been removed or stabilised. The landslides found in the South Wales valleys are often complex and at least seventeen contributory factors have been identified (Siddle and Bentley, 2000; Kenny and Cox, 2004; Donnelly, 2005; Taboga, 2010). These seventeen landslide factors can be grouped into five main categories: geological stratigraphy, geomorphological history, coal mining history, hydrology/hydrogeology and industrial development. Over the 44 year post Aberfan period, millions of pounds have been spent in colliery tip and landslide remediation projects throughout the South Wales valleys. The vast amount of research carried out by professional consultants for many of these landslide projects was at one time locked away in sensitive commercial reports out of the reach of teachers. However, since 2000, the National Museum of Wales has unlocked this information resource by inviting academics and consultants to publish articles

in a series of books in the "Landslide and Landslide Management" and "Urban Geology of Wales" series (Siddle *et al.*, 2000; Nichol *et al.*, 2004, Basset *et al.*, 2005, Bassett *et al.*, 2009). The teaching and learning exercise described in this paper is geographically based in the region of the Upper Taff and Rhondda Fawr valleys. The general context of the geological framework, physical geomorphology, mining history and environmental issues found in the Rhondda area of the Central Coalfield has been described in three papers by Brabham (2004, 2005, 2009a).

Teaching and learning programme

One of the biggest problems of modular structured undergraduate programmes is the compartmentalization of knowledge. The pressure on an undergraduate student is to pass each module, collect the marks in their portfolio and move onto the next module. Well-designed, multi-disciplinary, field-based teaching and learning exercises are vital in re-enforcing and applying previous knowledge across many modules, whilst also training students in research and best professional practice (Giles et. al., 2008). Ideally, before students can successfully tackle this multi-disciplinary quantitative geohazard analysis exercise, they should have previously studied level 4 and 5 modules in: geomorphology, geohazards, sedimentary geology, structural geology, natural resources, hydrogeology, data analysis and GIS.

The academic programme is divided into four separate stages as illustrated in Figure 1. The philosophy behind the design of this academic programme is not only multidisciplinary but also to cover all four aspects of research training for students described by Healey and Jenkins (2009).

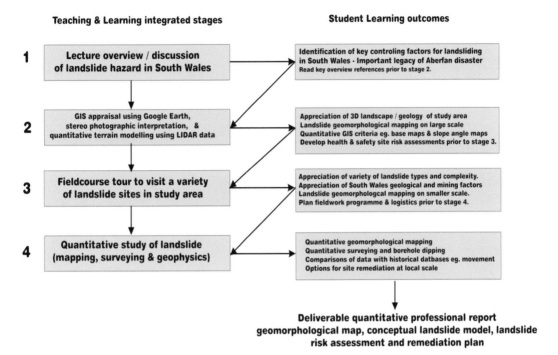

Figure 1. The four stages of the academic programme with student learning outcomes.

Stage 1

This introductory stage sets the scene for the whole programme by using the "research-tutored" and "research-led" approach (Healey and Jenkins, 2009). The student outcomes are a review of landslide types, basic geography / geology of the South Wales coalfield and a discussion on the key landsliding factors. An appreciation of the significance of the Aberfan disaster is re-enforced using archive video material followed by an interactive discussion. A landslide reading list is provided that students are required to read before commencing stage 2.

Stage 2

This stage involves use of geographical information systems to study both the regional and local context of key landslide sites. Depending on the GIS skills of the student cohort, this stage can range from simple web-based Google Earth studies

(Haslett, 2009) to full blown GIS terrain analysis using software programmes such as SURFER or ArcGIS (Figure 2). The two main outcomes of this stage for students are the production of a georeferenced base map which will be used in stage 4 and the completion of an individual health and safety risk analysis. Students must be made aware of the importance of completing a compulsory personal risk analysis before embarking on any field-based research programme.

Stage 3

This stage involves a one-day landslide tour commencing from Cardiff, travelling north up the A470 road by coach. A series of stops are made each with a strategic educational purpose (Figure 3). Geotechnical details for each stop can be found in the references provided, but the key educational point made at each stop is briefly described below.

Figure 2. Digital GIS terrain model of Blaencwm landslide created using Environment Agency LIDAR terrain data and Getmapping year 2000 digital air photography. © Crown copyright.

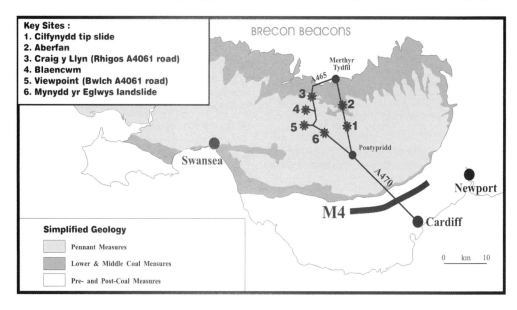

Figure 3. Fieldcourse map and key landslide site locations.

Site 1 Abercynon colliery tip slide, Cilfynydd (GR 309100,193350; Gallop and Bentley, 2000; Maddison, 2000). Very few un-remediated colliery tips now exist on the South Wales valley sides. Not only is Abercynon Colliery (1890-1988) tip at Cilfynydd an excellent example of one, but the remnants of a major flowslide that occurred in 1939, blocking both the original A470 road and River Taff can still be seen. Cilfynydd village inhabitants were also put under notice of evacuation in 1990 due to movements in the Albion colliery (1884-1966) tip high above the village. Emergency drainage wells were installed and monitoring measures are now in place. Cilfynydd is an excellent example of a mining village where indiscriminate colliery tipping on the valley sides has had a long standing geo-environmental legacy right up to the present day.

Site 2 Aberfan (GR 306570,200750; Penman, 2000 ; McLean and Johnes, 2000). Anybody studying geohazards in the UK should pay a visit to Aberfan. Today there are no visible remains of the massive tips responsible for the 1966 disaster. The protracted political wrangling over the Aberfan tip remediation is well chronicled by McLean and Johnes (2000). In the Aberfan disaster it is estimated that over 38,000m^3 of water saturated coal tip slurry from the

Merthyr Vale Colliery (1869-1989) was suddenly mobilised and flowed with tragic consequences downhill towards Aberfan village faster than a man could run. The educational strategy adopted at this sensitive site is to stop on the A4054 road opposite the village of Aberfan. Each student is given a photograph taken from the exact same geographical location in 1966. A poignant comparison of both contrasting views can be made and the disaster and its tragic consequences described (McLean and Johnes, 2000).

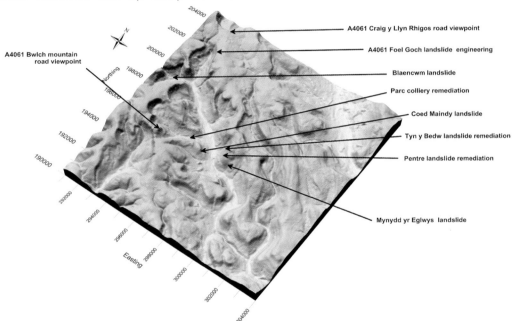

Figure 4. Key landslide sites and remediation projects in the Upper Rhondda Fawr valley.

Site 3 Craig y Lyn viewpoint (GR: 292500, 203100, Chambers, 2000). The A4061 Rhigos mountain road was built in the 1920s to improve inter-valley communication. The road has a long history of intermittent closure due to many landslide events and Chambers (2000) describes the ongoing monitoring programme for the road. The summit viewpoint at Craig y Llyn provides outstanding views of the regional geological and geomorphological setting and it also overlooks Tower Colliery which was the last deep coal mine operational in Wales (1864-

2008; Brabham, 2009a). In 1989 rock netting was installed to stop the constant rockfalls of Pennant Sandstone onto the road. In 1990 the A4061 suffered a major landslide event closing the road for over a year. The multi-million pound heavy engineering rock anchor design constructed to remediate the 1990 Foel Goch landslide can also be visited without difficulty on the descent into the Rhondda Fawr valley (Figure 5).

75

Figure 5. A4061 Foel Goch landslide remediation.

Figure 6. A4061 Bwlch mountain road viewpoint.

Site 4 Blaencwm Landslide (GR 291900,198750; Siddle, 2000). Blaencwm landslide is best viewed from a public footpath starting from the bus turning circle located at the furthest extent of Blaencwm village. The landslide area is the property of the Coal Authority and the backscarp is a potentially dangerous location. Blaencwm village has long history of coal mining from the Glenrhondda and Tydraw colleries that closed in 1968 and 1963 respectively. This huge and complex landslide developed in 1989 after a sudden failure of the Pennant Sandstone backscarp. It is estimated that 750,000m³ of rock was involved in the failure moving at 710mm per day. The village was at one time under severe landslide risk and an emergency evacuation plan was devised. The landslide is currently under constant remote monitoring using ground monitoring equipment with dial up links to a central data processing system at the offices of Halcrow Ltd in Cardiff. The huge scale of this landslide can be emphasised and the multi-million pound economics of remediation on such a scale can be appreciated. The remediation strategy adopted at Blaencwm has been to improve the site drainage using flexible drainage systems. At this location the link between rainfall and ground movement rates can be made to students.

Site 5 Bwlch Mountain road viewpoint (GR: 293950,194600). This dramatic viewpoint (Figure 6) provides views of obvious glacial geomorphology and the urban housing in its landscape context. From this point, views of major landslide remediation projects such as Park colliery (1864-1966) tip, Tyn y Bedw colliery (1876-1935) tip, Coed Maindy and Pentre landslides can be seen (Jones, 2000; Brabham, 2004). A contrast can be made between the harsh early 1990's heavy engineering of the Pentre landslide remediation and the softer environmentally-sensitive remediation strategy of the Tyn yr Bedw remediation carried out over a decade later.

Figure 7. Mynydd yr Eglwys landslide illustrating the hazard potential to modern housing at Meadow Walk.

Site 6 Mynydd yr Eglwys landslide (GR: 297800,195550, Taboga, 2010) Mynydd yr Eglwys landslide (MYE) is a recent deep-seated compound landslide that occurred in the Autumn of 1998 after a prolonged period of heavy rainfall. There is no coach access near to the landslide but it can be clearly viewed by parking on the Gelli industrial estate. If one wishes to walk up from Gelli village, there is safe public footpath access near to the landside from behind Meadow Walk (Figure 7). This landslide has been the subject of an intense Cardiff University PhD research project and to date has not had any major remediation undertaken except for some minor drainage improvements. The landslide has reactivated ancient debris slides which now threaten a major modern housing estate and the owners of houses in Meadow Walk have great difficulty in selling their properties because of the landslide risk.

The coach tour can return to Cardiff by travelling down the Rhondda Fawr valley to Pontypridd. On travelling through Porth, note can be made of a recent major road engineering project where landslide stabilisation and risk analysis was part of the engineering design (Campton *et al.*, 2009).

Stage 4

This final stage of the programme involves training students how to undertake a research study of an active landslide. This follows the "research-based" and "research-orientated" approach described by Healey and Jenkins (2009). Over the past four years the focus of research attention has been the Mynydd yr Eglwys landslide as it is an active landslide with good access, on a manageable mapping scale, with minimal health and safety risks for students and with no significant remediation undertaken apart from some minor drainage improvements.

Stage 2 of this programme will have provided students with a georeferenced base map of the study site. Students should have realised that conventional Ordnance Survey maps are often inadequate as base maps for mapping active landslides. Modern georeferenced air photographs or shaded relief images produced from Environment Agency LIDAR data are far superior. The key skills in landslide research training that students need to learn are:

1. Geomorphological mapping: A geomorphological map of the landslide is created by carefully walking over the site, usually with a handheld GPS for 10m accuracy ground positioning (Figure 8). Geomorphological features such as cliff faces, rock outcrops, rotated blocks, tension fissures, compressional folding, topographic lobes, coal tips, mine adits, spring lines etc. are all mapped onto a LIDAR derived base map (Figure 9).

Figure 8. Students undertaking a geomorphological mapping exercise.

2. Surveying: Students need to learn basic surveying skills using an EDM system to draw a centimetre accurate topographic cross section through the landslide and measure accurate slope angles (Figure 10).

3. Hydrogeology: On-site boreholes are dipped to provide information on water table depths. Boreholes sheared by ground movement are also indicators of the depth to the slip surface (Figure 11).

The primary objective of the PhD project is to research the use of novel techniques in landslide analysis. These include both stereo photogrammetry from a digital camera housed on a tethered Helium balloon (Figure 13) and a variety of geophysical methods.

Electrical resistivity, Self Potential, Induced Polarization and Electromagnetic mapping have been used. Student groups have been exposed to these research techniques and geophysical data is incorporated by students into their conceptual model of the landside.

The investigation techniques above provide the student with a technical snaphot of the landslide at the time of the survey. However, landslides in South Wales (as opposed to sudden colliery tip flowslides) often move relatively rapidly on initiation, but the rate of movement slows down through time. There are also seasonal variations in the ground movement rates, with winter rainfall increasing and summer drought slowing down the ground movement rate.

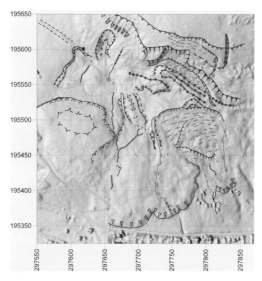

Figure 9. Geomorphological map of Mynydd yr Eglwys landslide plotted on a LIDAR base map (Taboga, 2010).

The primary objective of the PhD project is to research the use of novel techniques in landslide analysis. These include both stereo photogrammetry from a digital camera housed on a tethered Helium balloon (Figure 13) and a variety of geophysical methods. Electrical resistivity, Self Potential, Induced Polarization and Electromagnetic mapping have been used. Student groups have been exposed to these research techniques and

geophysical data is incorporated by students into their conceptual model of the landside.

Figure 10. Use of EDM instrument to construct a topographic cross section.

Figure 11. Students measuring depth to water table at Mynydd yr Eglwys landslide.

The investigation techniques above provide the student with a technical snaphot of the landslide at the time of the survey. However, landslides in South Wales (as opposed to sudden colliery tip flowslides) often move relatively rapidly on initiation, but the rate of movement slows down through time. There are also seasonal variations in the ground movement rates, with winter rainfall increasing and summer drought slowing down the ground movement rate.

The site conceptual model

Students must be made aware of current best practice used for both research and in the professional geo-environmental industries. Students must be aware of and follow British Standards (BS5930) relating to site investigation and use standard SI units and Ordnance Survey grid references for all their field measurements. The two key components of any final report are an accurate geomorphological map using standard symbols plus a site conceptual model. A conceptual model is now a widely-recognised tool used in geo-environmental studies. It can take many forms, but in the context of landslide research, it is normally a diagrammatic technical summary of the site, either drawn as a 2D cross-section plotted to scale or a 3D technical diagram. Students must also be aware of the limitations and inaccuracies in their landslide model and propose future research strategies to fill in the holes in their knowledge base.

Temporal studies

Students need to appreciate the temporal nature of landslides. The only way they can do this is by comparing the data collected during their particular survey with a database of previous data. This is where a parallel PhD research programme is invaluable in improving the teaching and learning experience of the students. In this project, a library of temporal data is provided via a number of sources e.g. permanent survey points. Experience from this project has shown that wooden pegs do not last very long on Urban Welsh hillsides due to sheep and inquisitive children. Professional rock anchor markers have now been used on the MYE landslide. These survey points are regularly re-occupied using a research DGPS surveying system to a sub 5mm accuracy

(Taboga, 2010). Students can compare the x,y,z position of each marker with those of previous years to assess the amount and rate of ground movement.

Figure 12. CUROP-funded student David James using a DGPS surveying system to locate ground anchor points.

Hydrogeology and hydrology

An historical record of local rainfall is currently provided by automatic local weather stations at Treherbert, Blaencwm landslide and Nantgwyddon Landfill sites. However the rainfall data has proven to be not 100% reliable, with regular data drop outs. We are currently investigating the prospect of installing our own weather station at a local secure site.

To constantly monitor groundwater levels on site permanent data loggers have been installed in boreholes. These data loggers monitor water levels every hour and can be left for months before downloading the data to a laptop PC. The loggers provide a temporal record of borehole groundwater levels which can be correlated with rainfall.

A library of resources used in this project has been set up by the authors using the BLACKBOARD WebCT, E-learning system. Students can access the data remotely via a web link and download articles, historical datafiles and site imagery. Setting up a BLACKBOARD electronic resource involves the teacher in a great deal of initial effort, but it has long term rewards in that it only needs to be updated every year. Previously used shared library-based paper resources often resulted in competitive squabbling amongst students and required every student to physically be on campus to complete the project write-up as a professional report. As the MSc course has a percentage of part-time students on day release, use of BLACKBOARD WebCT has meant that these part-time students can access the data from their home or company base.

Figure 13. Students working on MYE landslide as viewed by a digital camera mounted on a Helium balloon platform (photo: Nick Russill, Terradat (UK) Ltd).

Mutual benefits of linking teaching and research

Experience from this academic programme has shown that linking teaching with a field-based PhD research programme has many benefits. The PhD student has acted as a field demonstrator training students in the use of expensive research equipment. The Cardiff University Research Opportunities Programme (CUROP) has also supported this landslide research by funding two undergraduate students over 8 weeks during the summer vacation. This CUROP grant allowed undergraduate students to shadow the PhD student and learn how to use expensive research equipment.

All the above exercises have provided a database of landslide information that can be accessed by students each year. The EPSRC PhD grant only covered the employment and field expenses of Ms. Taboga and the majority of research fieldwork was performed solely by the paper's authors. Whilst the topographic surveying can be performed by two people, geophysical surveying requires carrying heavy equipment and cables on site. To carry out a 340m long electrical resistivity survey onto a landslide requires a great deal of manual labour. When student parties are engaged in the research programme it allows large scale surveys to be performed that would be virtually impossible to carry out by two people. Therefore the mutual benefits of combining teaching and research cannot be denied.

Summary

This paper describes a four-stage educational programme to undertake a quantitative study of landslide hazard and risk at a site in the Rhondda Fawr valley in South Wales.

Although Cardiff University has visited Rhondda landslides on fieldtrips since 1999, this enhanced educational project has evolved over the last four years in conjunction with an EPSRC CASE PhD research study undertaken by Alessia Taboga with industrial sponsorship by Terradat (UK) Ltd based in Cardiff Bay. The teaching and learning programme builds on precursor modules and uses key skills such as field-mapping and GIS to achieve its successful outcome. Students learn research best practice and that quantitative geohazard field investigation is multidisciplinary. This educational project is an excellent example of the mutual benefits of linking industrially-sponsored academic research with teaching and learning programmes.

Acknowledgements

The authors acknowledge the role of Professor Charles Harris in the early years of this landslide educational and research programme before his retirement. Alessia Taboga is funded by an EPSRC CASE studentship. Nick Russill of Terradat (UK) Ltd is the industrial supervisor of Ms. Taboga and has also contributed much to the geophysical research programme. Howard Siddle of Halcrow Ltd is the acknowledged expert on South Wales landslides and their remediation and the idea of a Rhondda landslide fieldcourse came from an Engineering Group of the Geological Society field weekend led by Howard. Howard has been extremely supportive along with other Halcrow staff, especially Malcolm Turner throughout this project. Topcon supplied the DGPS surveying equipment through a generous educational support programme and Leighton Davies of Topcon (Cardiff office) is thanked for his training support. RCT council has supplied conventional landslide surveying data and Amgen Cymru rainfall data from their landfill sites. The Cardiff University Research Opportunities Programme (CUROP) is also thanked for supporting two B.Sc. students David James and Owen Davies during this landslide research.

REFERENCES

BASSETT, M.G., DEISLER, V. K., NICHOL, D. 2005. (eds) Urban Geology in Wales II, National Museum of Wales Geological Series No.24, Cardiff. 262 pp.

BASSETT, M.G., BOULTON, H., NICHOL, D., 2009. (eds.) Urban Geology in Wales III, National Museum of Wales Geological Series 26, Cardiff. 199pp.

BRABHAM, P.J. 2004. The Rhondda Valleys: Using GIS to visualize a variety of geological issues in an intensely mined area.. In: NICHOL, D., BASSETT, M.G., and DEISLER, V.K. (eds.) Urban Geology in Wales, National Museum of Wales Geological Series No.23, Cardiff. pp. 222-233.

BRABHAM, P.J. 2005. The Rhondda valleys: Using GIS to visualise the rise and fall of coal mining and its industrial legacy. In: BASSETT, M.G, DEISLER, V.K and NICHOL, D. (eds) Urban Geology in Wales II, National Museum of Wales Geological Series No.24, Cardiff. pp.193-204.

BRABHAM, P.J. 2009a. The Central Valleys of South Wales: Using GIS to visualize the geology, landscape and coal mining legacy. In BASSETT, M.G. and BOULTON, H. NICHOL, D. (eds), Urban Geology in Wales III, National Museum of Wales Geological Series 26, Cardiff. pp.150-161.

BRABHAM, P.J. 2009b. Undergraduate field-based project training exercises and Masters' level vocational training projects in Applied Environmental Geoscience, using study sites in South Wales. In *Linking research and Teaching in Higher education*, Haslett, S., Rowlands, H (eds.) Proceedings of the Newport NEXUS conference, Centre for excellence in Learning and Teaching. Special Publication No.1, pp.137-145.

CAMPTON, A.L., LEVISIANOU, M., MALIPHANT, P.C., WILLIAMS, C.R. 2009. Porth Relief Road : Overcoming engineering geology challenges through effective partnership. In BASSETT, M.G., BOULTON, H. NICHOL, D. (eds), Urban Geology in Wales III, National Museum of Wales Geological Series 26, Cardiff. pp..55-64.

CHAMBERS, S. 2000. A4061 Rhigos mountain road: road management in a landslide area. In: SIDDLE, H.J, BROMHEAD, H.J., and BASSETT, M.G. (eds) Landslide and landslide management in South Wales. Cardiff: National Museum of Wales, pp. 94-97.

CONWAY, B. W., FORSTER, A., NORTHMORE, K. J., BARCLAY, W. J. 1980. South Wales Coalfield landslip survey. London: Institute of Geological Sciences. Special Surveys Division. Engineering Geology Unit, Report No EG 80/4. Volume 1 (text), pp. 218; Volume 2 (catalogue), pp. 131.

DONNELLY, L.J. 2005. Fault reactivation in South Wales and the affects on ground stability. In: BASSETT, M.G, DEISLER, V.K and NICHOL, D. (eds) Urban Geology in Wales II, National Museum of Wales Geological Series No.24, Cardiff. pp.99- 117.

FORSTER, A., JENKINS, G.O., 2005, The assessment of landslide hazard potential as a guide to land use and planning in the South Wales coalfield. In: BASSETT, M.G, DEISLER, V.K, NICHOL, D. (eds) Urban Geology in Wales II, National Museum of Wales Geological Series No.24, Cardiff. pp.81-87.

GALLOP, M.C., BENTLEY, S. P. 2000. The geomorphology of the Clifynydd flow slide. In: SIDDLE, H.J, BROMHEAD, H.J., BASSETT, M.G. (eds) Landslide and landslide management in South Wales. Cardiff: National Museum of Wales, pp. 36-39.

GILES, D., WHITWORTH, M., POULSOM, A., 2008 The development of fieldwork problem based exercises in the applied sciences. Planet, No.20, pp, 37-40.

HASLETT, S.K. 2009. Prior use of Google Earth by Undergraduate Geography students, Planet, No.22, Higher Education Authority, pp 43-47.

HEALEY, M., JENKINS, A. 2009 Developing students as researchers. In *Linking Research and Teaching in Higher education*, Haslett, S. K. and Rowlands, H (eds.) Proceedings of the Newport NEXUS conference, Centre for excellence in Learning and Teaching. Special Publication No.1, pp 7-11.

JONES, D.B. 2000. Pentre landslides: stabilization by earthworks. In: SIDDLE, H.J, BROMHEAD, H.J., and BASSETT, M.G. (eds) Landslide and landslide management in South Wales. Cardiff: National Museum of Wales, pp. 103-105

KENNY, R.J., COX, S.J. 2004. Geo-environmental considerations for developments in the South Wales coalfield. In: NICHOL, D., BASSETT, M.G., and DEISLER, V.K. (eds) Urban Geology in Wales, National Museum of Wales Geological Series No.23, Cardiff. . pp189-196.

MADDISON, J.D. 2000. Albion colliery tip and landslide: deep drainage by bored drains. In: SIDDLE, H.J, BROMHEAD, H.J., and BASSETT, M.G. (eds) Landslide and landslide management in South Wales. Cardiff: National Museum of Wales, pp. 100-103.

McLEAN, I., JOHNES, M. 2000. Aberfan, government and disasters, Welsh Academic Press, 274pp.

NICHOL, D., BASSETT, M.G. DEISLER, V.K. 2004. (eds.) Urban Geology in Wales, National Museum of Wales Geological Series No.23, Cardiff. 256 pp.

MARSHAK, S. 2007. Earth: Portrait of a Planet (3rd Edition), W.W.Norton, 896pp.

PENMAN, A.D.M. 2000. The Aberfan flow slide, In: Siddle, H.J, Bromhead, H.J., and Bassett, M.G. (eds) Landslide and landslide management in South Wales. Cardiff: National Museum of Wales, pp. 62-68.

SIDDLE, H. J. 2000. Blaencwm Landslide, Rhondda Fawr. In: SIDDLE, H.J, BROMHEAD, H.J., and BASSETT, M.G. (eds) Landslide and landslide management in South Wales. Cardiff: National Museum of Wales, pp. 9-14.

SIDDLE, H. J., BENTLEY, S. P. 2000. A brief history of landslide research in South Wales. In: SIDDLE, H.J, BROMHEAD, H.J., and BASSETT, M.G. (eds.) Landslide and landslide management in South Wales. Cardiff: National Museum of Wales, pp. 9-14.

SIDDLE, H.J. BROMHEAD, H.J., BASSETT, M.G. 2000. (eds) Landslide and landslide management in South Wales. Cardiff: National Museum of Wales, Geological series No.18, 116pp.

TABOGA, A. 2010. The development of high-resolution geophysical investigation and monitoring of landslides with examples from the South Wales Coalfield. Unpublished PhD thesis, School of Earth and Ocean Sciences, Cardiff University.

Enhancing Research-Teaching Links in Higher Education
Simon K. Haslett and Hefin Rowlands (eds)
Proceedings of the Newport NEXUS Conference
Centre for Excellence in Learning and Teaching
Special Publication, No. 3, 2010, pp. 83-91
ISBN 978-1-899274-43-7

University of Wales, Newport

Prifysgol Cymru, Casnewydd

Ensuring student engagement in 3D virtual learning environments.

Joe Wan[1], Mike Reddy[2] and David Longman[3]

[1]Centre for Excellence in Learning and Teaching, University of Wales, Newport, Lodge Road, Caerleon, South Wales, NP18 3QT. Email: joe.wan@newport.ac.uk

[2]Newport Business School, University of Wales, Newport, Lodge Road, Caerleon, South Wales, NP18 3QT. Email: mike.ready@newport.ac.uk

[3]Newport School of Education, University of Wales, Newport, Lodge Road, Caerleon, South Wales, NP18 3QT. Email: david.longman@newport.ac.uk

Abstract

Internet and Web 2.0 technologies have contributed significantly to distance learning and completely changed how people interact online, and in turn, the role of the tutor as facilitator is given a new emphasis. According to the theory of Communities of Practice and the model of Situated Learning, learning is largely a social practice rather than something individuals do. With the increasing pressure to deliver learning at a distance, one particular technology, 3D Virtual Learning Environments (VLEs), is being investigated as a means to supplement campus-based learning because 3D VLEs enable a possibility for social engagement which other technologies do not. Research to date about student engagement and learning in 3D VLEs has tended to rely on anecdotal or epithetic evidence. There has been little measurement employed in the initial design of experiments and which have tended to be very technologically focused. Lots of assessments of learning were actually about assessment of technology. Even if there was initial measurement of educational outcomes and there was less technology-focus, experiments might not be scalable to other VLEs. In order to explore the opportunities for social engagement as well as technical engagement in 3D VLEs, this paper will investigate student engagement within virtual learning communities through the exploration of the proposed ideas about narrative and avatars, i.e. narrative creation is an imaginative and cognitive process and essential to student engagement; avatars are the animated agents that connect sociability and interactivity. In 3D VLEs, there is the possibility for community to be re-introduced that other technologies may have stripped out. In addition, the role of the tutor in virtual learning communities is further developed as a co-participant rather than simply a facilitator because in addition to the need for a tutor to provide scaffolding or even intervene in open-ended VLEs (e.g. Second Life) there is also peer negotiated and self-directed learning. A review of literature and directly observed case studies is performed. A model of learning that emphasizes an individual's role within a socially regulated community will be used to analyse the existing use of virtual environments in order to measure different styles of engagement. As a result, this paper concludes that narrative is the mechanism that binds communities together and that avatars are the mechanism by which a personal narrative is implemented.

Introduction

The ubiquitous nature of Internet and Web 2.0 technologies (*e.g.* wikis, blogs, video online, social networks) has contributed significantly to distance learning and completely changed how people interact online, and in turn, a new learning paradigm evolves where tutors are facilitators. However, some social elements in traditional learning have been stripped out by the use of technologies. Lack of synchronous communication and multi-user online role playing activities in Web 2.0 may potentially reduce students' experience and efficiencies in terms of Community of Practice. As a result, there is a push for the development of 3D VLEs, *e.g.* Second Life. The social elements once diminished are now embedded in 3D VLEs via avatars. The idea of tutor has been put back in and redressed because communication between students and between students and tutors is essential to collaborative learning (Veerman, Else 2001).

MIMESIS system, a 3D interactive narrative-based learning environment, created at NC State University, and a Second Life workshop for Religious Studies students at Newport School of Education will be evaluated based on the theory of Community of Practice.

Furthermore, when analysing student engagement, traditional research focuses solely on the tangible aspect of 3D VLEs, *e.g.* attendance. However, "participating in a learning community may have a salutary effect on academic performance" (Zhao and Kuh 2004) and this is regarding the quality of student engagement. Hence, it requires to have a balanced view and take both tangible and intangible aspects into consideration, through the "inner eye of the soul" (Ryan 2001), *i.e.* narrative; and the "physical eye of the body" (Ryan 2001), *i.e.* avatar, because a narrative is the glue that binds the community together and the way by which a Community of Practice develops; an avatar is the mechanism by which a narrative is implemented in-world.

Social Element and Student Engagement

Student Engagement in Traditional Learning Environments

According to the existing research (*i.e.* (Stovall 2003) (Krause, Coates 2008) (Bulger et al. 2008)), student engagement can be defined as students' willingness to participate in purposeful academic activities over a period of time, which in turn positively contributes to expected learning outcome .

Quantitative measurement, *i.e.* attendance, dominated the way of how student engagement was measured before online learning gained significant ground (Douglas, Alemanne 2007). However, engagement and participation are fundamentally different. Although participation is one main indicator and has direct impact on student engagement (Douglas 2008), the non-quantifiable factor behind it, *i.e.* motivation, has been largely ignored. Motivation is defined as "an internal state or condition that activates behaviour and gives it direction (Huitt 2001)" (Beer 2010). Motivation is derived from students' mutual engagement in the common learning activities (Wenger 1998). This leads to the theory of Community of Practice which has gained its popularity in recent years.

Accordingly to Lave and Wenger (1991), learning is largely a social practice rather than something that individuals do. In other words, Communities of practice are "groups of people who share a concern or a passion for something they do and learn how to do it better as they interact regularly" (Wenger 2006). Communities of Practice can be regarded as "self-organizing systems" (Smith 2009) and the process of collective learning within them can be deemed as Self Regulated Community of Learning (SRCL), *i.e.* socially mediated rather than purely Self Regulated Learning (SRL), because SRL is "in relation to the environment" (Wan and Reddy 2009). Furthermore, according to Vygotsky (1978), a learner "first becomes able to subordinate her behavior to rules in group play and only later does voluntary self regulation of behavior arise as an internal function" (Vygotsky 1978). Hence, "[t]heoretically and conceptually, the learning community appears to be a potentially powerful educational practice" (Zhao and Kuh 2004), because "[t]he increased opportunities afforded by learning communities for peer learning and interaction allow for the development of richer, complex ways of thinking and knowing so that students learn at a deeper level (Bransford, Brown and Cocking 2000)" (Zhao and Kuh 2004).

Recent analysis by Zhao and Kuh (2004) about first-year and senior students from 365 four-year institutions also indicates that participation in a learning community may have positive impact on students' academic performance. For instance, "seniors with a learning community experience had higher grades compared with those who did not participate in a learning community at some point during college" (Zhao and Kuh 2004), but "no difference in the grades of first-year students" (Zhao and Kuh 2004). This finding resounds deeply with the learnablity issues raised by Wan and Reddy (2009). Because according to the level descriptors of Northern Ireland credit Accumulation and Transfer System (NICATS), as the level goes down, students tend to be less capable of SRL, thus require socially mediated learning, namely SRCL. Although SRCL does not have immediate impact on the first-year student's academic performance in the above analysis, learning communities have stronger impact on first year students than for seniors because "a learning community is associated with higher levels of academic effort, academic integration, and active and collaborative learning" (Zhao and Kuh 2004).

The model of Situated Learning rests in Community of Practice and is opposite to abstract learning, and learning occurs in a co-construction process in a contextualized environment (Lave, Wenger 1991)(Smith 2009). Situated Learning is directly related to the concept of narrative, which is defined as "a story that is created in a constructive format (as a work of writing, speech, poetry, prose, pictures, song, motion pictures, video games, theatre or dance) that describes a sequence of fictional or non-fictional events" (Wikimedia 2010). Narratives are everywhere. For example, students choose universities based on selected narratives in various formats, and subsequently being guided by other educational narratives throughout their learning process. These narratives are external to students, because traditional learning is didactic and instructional by nature. Although story-based Learning environments harness the creation of both formal and informal learning communities, the contextualized learning environment in traditional learning setting is created by tutors rather than by students themselves. Therefore, there is a potential for students to have more involvement in narrative creating process in order to "further develop their identity and discover their voice as well as to integrate what they are learning into their world view and other academic and social experiences" (Zhao and Kuh 2004).

Narrative-centred approach has significant impact on student engagement. In turn, it leads to in-depth student learning and individual development and educational effectiveness (Zhao and Kuh 2004) .

However, traditional teaching and learning have limitations, because the population of students are getting increasingly large and people are economically restricted to where they can go and when they can learn due to their available time and geographic locations. Therefore, there is a demand for distance learning to be conducted over the Internet.

Student Engagement with Web 2.0

As discussed above, student engagement is entirely a social process. "Engagement is seen to comprise active and collaborative learning, participation in challenging academic activities, formative communication with academic staff, involvement in enriching educational experiences, and feeling legitimated and supported by university learning communities (Coates 2007)" (Beer 2010).

The ubiquitous nature of Internet and Web 2.0 technologies (*e.g.* wikis, blogs, video online, social networks) has contributed significantly to distance learning and completely changed how people interact online, and in turn, a new learning paradigm evolves where tutors are facilitators. Nevertheless, current distance education still "has more in common with traditional classroom-based instruction than it does with what distance education can become" (Bronack, Riedl and Tashner 2006), because distance learning is still largely instructional.

"Learning occurs first on the social level and next on the individual one" (Vygotsky 1978). However, some social elements in traditional learning have been stripped out by the use of technologies. Lack of synchronous communication (e.g. face-to-face interaction between tutor and students, student and student) and multi-user online role playing activities in Web 2.0 may potentially reduce students' experience and efficiencies for learning. As shown in Figure 1, traditional learning and web 2.0 learning each represents a quarter of the entire learning scope. Blended Learning is "the organic integration of thoughtfully selected and complementary face-to-face and online approaches and technologies" (Garrison, Vaughan 2008). However, Blended Learning is still unable to cope with the entire spectrum of distance learning, and in turn there is a push for the development of 3D Virtual Learning Environments, e.g. Second Life. As a result, those social elements once diminished are now embedded in 3D VLEs via avatars. Blended Online Learning caters the needs of distance learning because it is the combined effort of all sorts of technologies, including Web 2.0 and 3D VLEs, which covers almost the entire scope of online learning, as show in Figure 1.

One important feature of learning in 3D VLEs is that the idea of tutor has been put back in and redressed because communication between students and between students and tutors is essential to collaborative learning (Veerman, Else 2001). In addition, recent analysis by Zhao and Kuh (2004) about first-year and senior students from 365 four-year institutions shows that for both classes, members within a learning community were "strongly linked with active and collaborative learning and interaction with faculty members" (Zhao and Kuh 2004). As a result, tutors should be active participants (or co-participants) rather than simply facilitators in Blended Online Learning and 3D VLEs are more capable of fostering learning communities compared with the employment of Web 2.0 alone. This is called "3rd-party Directed Learning (3DL), where the tutor and VLEs co-exist" (Wan and Reddy 2009) and learning is regulated by both learning environments and virtual learning communities. The transition from Web 2.0 to the integration of Web 2.0 and 3D VLEs can be deemed as techno fix for techno problems.

In 3D VLEs, educational narrative is defined as "story-telling for purposes of education, training, or entertainment in which a user interacts with a computer system to experience a story as an active participant" (Young, Riedl 2003) and is usually created by a tutor. This is similar to Massively Multiplayer Online Role-playing Games (MMORPGs) which is plot-driven and narratives are pre-defined. It is worth noting that the word narrative in this paper refers narrative in a non-traditional sense, i.e. non-textual narrative, because MMPORGs and 3D VLEs by nature are non-textual worlds and here, non-textual refers to that there is no deliberate design on the part of somebody, rather than saying that letters or words are omitted.

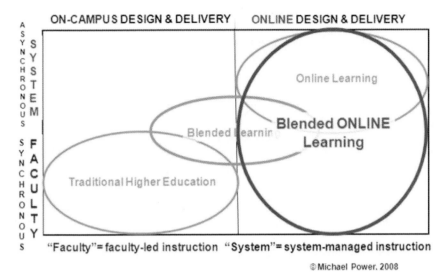

Figure 1. The relative position of Blended Online Learning (Power 2008).

Student Engagement in 3D VLEs

When analysing student engagement, traditional research focuses solely on the tangible aspect of 3D VLEs, *e.g.* attendance. However, "participating in a learning community may have a salutary effect on academic performance" (Zhao and Kuh 2004) and this is regarding the quality of student engagement. Hence, it requires to have a balanced view and take both tangible and intangible aspects into consideration, through the "inner eye of the soul" (Ryan 2001), *i.e.* narrative; and the "physical eye of the body" (Ryan 2001), *i.e.* avatar, because a narrative is the glue that binds the community together and the way by which a community of practice develops; an avatar is the mechanism by which a narrative is implemented in-world.

Narrative

Narrative creation is a (meta-)cognitive process, is essential to student engagement. When the system revolves around human input, as in the case of 3D VLEs, "every visit to the system actualizes a different narrative path" (Ryan 2001). Eventually all such sequential events will fit the looser pattern of episodic narrative. Therefore, the efficacy of student engagement in 3D VLEs will be multiplied.

As discussed in the previous section, built-in narrative is vital but external to students because they are tutor-created. However, this is only one side of the coin. In 3D VLEs, Second life in particular, narratives are co-created by students and narrative co-creation process is essential to the development of Community of Practice. This also represents the shift in higher education setting, *i.e.* from instructional learning to 3rd-party directed SRL, "where learning content can either be defined by the environment (*e.g.* a tutor or a thematic game), or by the students themselves (*i.e.* user generated content)" (Wan and Reddy 2009) or both. In other words, the advantage 3D VLEs has over Web 2.0 is the holistic approach of social interaction, because "learning communities operationalize a constructivist approach to knowledge (Cross 1998), whereby knowledge is not simply "discovered" but is socially constructed" (Zhao and Kuh 2004). Therefore, the efficacy of the so-called guided learning environments (*e.g.* MiMESIS) need to be re-evaluated based on the theory of Community of Practice, *i.e.* do gated or semi-gated learning environments promote or hinder the development of SRCL?

The activities in both MMORPGs and 3D VLEs have heuristic value because "the creation and exploration of imaginary worlds can be an instrument of self-discovery" (Ryan 2001). Nevertheless, 3D VLEs have more potential for higher education than MMORPGs do due to their open-ended nature. It is noteworthy to mention that the word, open-ended, is a relative term because Second Life is actually a platform and has the capability to host both gated environments such as MMORPGs and educational games, and open-ended virtual learning environments.

The difference between narrative in gated learning environment (*e.g.* interactive narrative-based systems and MMORPGs) and open ended learning environment (*e.g.* Second Life) is that the former has predefined narratives which has "a structured sequence of events" (Young, Riedl 2003); the latter offers "the ability for users to create their own narratives from the ground up" (Meadows 2008) and is "a prospective point of view, without knowledge of their outcome" (Ryan 2001). The depth of student engagement in both is accomplished by plot-driven. However, the former is a story unfolds; the latter is mainly about the co-creation process of a story.

In addition, although an interactive narrative system creates structured narrative at run time by taking "a user's ability, interests, previous experience and other contextual factors" (Young, Riedl 2003) into account, it has significant disadvantages compared with open-ended environment such as Second Life. For instance, MIMESIS system, a 3D interactive narrative-based learning environment, created at NC State University, solely focuses on the interaction between student and the computer mediated learning environment, thus has ignored the social aspects of learning, i.e. "community building, and social interaction" (Hoog, Falkner and Seifried 2007). In other words, MIMESIS system might be a success from IT perspective, but it is definitely a failure in reference to the theory of Community of Practice, because it fails to meet the basic requirement of student engagement, *e.g.* active and collaborative learning, formative communication with tutors, as addressed at the beginning of section 2.2.

Although narrative co-creating process is the core of student engagement, the importance of the design of 3D VLEs should not be overlooked, because when a student enters a 3D VLE, she has to deal with a world that has already had some sort of built-in narrative though the build-in narrative is not aimed at any specific individual. Like 'Alice in Wonderland', a student walks into a built-in narrative script or story and automatically becomes a character. She cannot be fully engaged with the virtual environment until the boundary of the first person and third person perspectives gets blurred or diminished. This will be further explained in the next section with the use of avatar. As a result, a tutor is responsible for creating such an inspiring environment for students, especially for those who are novice or naïve. The observation of a Second Life workshop for Religious Studies students at Newport School of Education in December 2009 further proves the importance of design, because the virtual religious sites visited by the students are unable to foster learning community due to lack of required built-in narratives. After all, those virtual sites are not designed for educational purpose.

A 3D VLE such as Second Life is a virtual world that "stretch[es] in space, exist[s] in time, and serve[s] as habitat for a population of animate agents" (Ryan 2001). Hence, it is an ideal place for academic practice, theoretically the expected depth of student engagement can be achieved because the aforementioned three dimensions "correspond to what have long been recognized as the three basic components of narrative grammar: setting, plot, and characters" (Ryan 2001).

Moreover, what 3D VLEs are really unique about is Multi-user Online Role Play via avatars which contribute to both spatio-temporal and emotional immersions and subsequently shared experience.

Avatar

Avatar is "an interactive, social representation of a user" (Meadows 2008), the animated agent that connects sociability and interactivity. Some literature defines avatar as the virtual representation of self. However, according to Ignatius, the self is "an indivisible 'compound of body and soul' (Exercises, 136)" (Ryan 2001). In 3D VLEs, body has been conceptualized as being virtual as "we would experience an expansion of our physical and sensory powers; leave our bodies and see ourselves from the outside; adopt new identities" (Ryan 2001) in the form of 3D avatars. An avatar by itself has far less meaning than a 'self' does. Avatars allow us to observe the roles played by us through the lens of third person. Therefore, avatars are the virtual representation of the characters not ourselves, until the moment that the boundary of the first and third person perspectives gets blurred or diminished, strictly speaking, when emotional immersion is accomplished.

The increased level of immersion in 3D VLEs is due to the increased level of fidelity, because "3D virtual environments (VEs) make use of the third dimension to increase the participant's sense of reality" (Scheucher et al. 2009), namely the geographical metaphor which was a "defining element in computer games" (Aarseth 2001). 3D VLEs are "richly rendered general purpose platform[s]" (Balkin, Noveck 2006) through which "spatial representation and negotiation" (Aarseth 2001) is achieved. The 3D added value is accomplished by the employment of avatar, which is an additional layer of the communication in virtual worlds. In turn, community building is a direct result of increased self-awareness and awareness of others.

Avatars have a significant impact on virtual identity, because students will not engage in the process of learning unless they feel that they are engaged in the community of learning. Therefore, in 3D VLEs, "the motive is to define the boundaries of identity rather than the boundaries of land" (Meadows 2008) because "avatar is a specific persona, and different identity, of the driver" (Meadows 2008). Behavioural rituals "require specific sort of personalities" (Meadows 2008) and "give archetypes meaning and expression, and vice-versa. The visual representation that a person chooses for their avatar has

something to do with their role in the society" (Meadows 2008).

Some people claim that learners can be distracted from what intended to be as the focus because there are too many new experiences to be dealt with at once. Thus, 3D VLEs would not be effective learning environments if they were lack of familiar Real World features. Although this kind of "mimic ethos" (Kirriemuir 2007) has received lots of criticism over years, this view is not completely wrong or obsolete as it does have some positive impact on learning in 3D VLES, *e.g.* in the case of avatar appearance and virtual identity. Avatars can "present valuable identity information solely by appearance" (Schmeil, Eppler 2008) and affect "the quality of interaction between tutors and tutees" (Fedeli 2009), because the appearance of an avatar is one indication of students' perception of their tutor's professionalism, as research shows that students indeed re-evaluate their tutor based on her avatar appearance (Fedeli 2009). Simply put, real life appearance or similar will increase the trust and create instant affinity between students and their tutor. As suggested by Casanueva *et al.* that "the awareness of collaborators and their actions can be significantly enhanced by more realistic representations of persons" (Casanueva, Blake 2000). Furthermore, according to the poll done by Zogby International at the behest of the U.S. Congressional Internet Caucus Advisory Committee, 44.2% of the respondents prefer to "[k]eep me just about the same as I am" (Reuters 2008) regarding the question on their avatar appearance. In addition, real life appearance or similar can offset the confusion caused by the naming convention in Second Life. Naming convention in Second Life also has direct impact on virtual identity, but this will not be discussed here due to the focus of this paper.

Conclusion

Because most work done in 3D VLEs is still exploratory, so their efficacy for learning and teaching remains largely underexplored. In order to better understand the academic potential of 3D VLEs, Second Life in particular, it is essential to evaluate the factors that underlie student engagement.

Under the framework of the Self Regulated Community of Learning (SRCL), Narrative as Student Engagement (vice-versa) is one more step forward in guiding real practice in 3D VLEs and an addition to postmodern narrative theory. Narrative as Student Engagement is an attempt to close the gap between spatio-temporal and emotional immersions in 3D VLEs. Narrative as Student Engagement builds the sense of community. In turn, the sense of community improves the depth of student engagement.

3D VLEs such as Second Life has significant advantages over web 2.0, gated virtual learning environment and single-user virtual learning environments in terms of group building and collaborative learning. However, Blended Online Learning is the combined effort of all of them. User engagement is much easier to be achieved in 3D VLEs because they provide "an advanced level of social networking through the employment of avatars" (Kirriemuir 2007), and allow people to "act within a world and experience it from the inside" (Ryan 2001). Thus, narrative is the mechanism that glues the community together; avatars are the mechanism by which the concept of the community is reintroduced and a narrative is implemented in-world.

REFERENCES

AARSETH, E. 2001, "Allegories of space - The question of spatiality in computer games", [Online], . Available from: http://cybertext.hum.jyu.fi/articles/129.pdf. [April 30, 2010].

BALKIN, J. M., NOVECK, B.S. 2006, *The state of play: law, games, and virtual worlds,* New York University Press, New York.

BEER, C. 2010, *Student Engagement,* http://beerc.wordpress.com/2010/02/17/student-engagement/ edn, Col's Weblog.

BRANSFORD, J.D., BROWN, A.L., COCKING, P.R. (eds) 2000, *How people learn: brain, mind, experience, and school*, National Research Council/National Academy Press., Washington, DC.

BRONACK, S., RIEDL, R., TASHNER, J. 2006, "Learning in the zone: a social constructivist framework

for distance education in a 3-Dimensional virtual world", *Interactive Learning Environments,* vol. 14, no. 3, pp. 219-232.

BULGER, M.E., MAYER, R.E., ALMEROTH, K.C., BLAU, S.D. 2008, "Measuring learner engagement in computer-equipped college classrooms", *Journal of Educational Multimedia and Hypermedia,* vol. 17, no. 2, pp. 129-143.

CASANUEVA, J., BLAKE, E. 2000, "The effects of group collaboration on presence in a collborative virtual environment", *EGVE'00 – 6th Eurographics Workshop on Virtual Environments,* [Online], . Available from: http://pubs.cs.uct.ac.za/archive/00000285/01/CS00-07-00.pdf. [April 30, 2010].

COATES, H. 2007, "A model of online and general campus-based student engagement", *Assessment and Evaluation in Higher Education,* vol. 32, no. 2, pp. 121-141.

CROSS, K.P. 1998, "Why learning communities? Why now?", *About Campus,* vol. 4, no. 11.

DOUGLAS, I. 2008, "Measuring Participation in Internet Supported Courses", *Paper presented at the 2008 International Conference on Computer Science and Software Engineering, Wuhan, China,* .

DOUGLAS, I. AND ALEMANNE, N.D. 2007, "Measuring Student Participation and Effort", *Paper presented at the International Conference on Cognition and Exploratory Learning in Digital Age, Algarve, Portugal,* .

FEDELI, L. 2009, "Avatar-assisted learning: Second Life and the new challenges of online tutoring", [Online], . Available from: http://www.iicm.tugraz.at/home/cguetl/Conferences/ViWo/ViWo2009Workshop/finalpapers/ViWo2009Workshop_01.pdf. [January 10, 2010].

GARRISON, D.R., VAUGHAN, N.D. 2008, *Blended learning in higher education,* Jossey-Bass, San Francisco, CA.

HEFCW 2004, *Higher Education in Wales Credit Specification and Guidance,* HEFCW, Cardiff, Wales.

HOOG, J., FALKNER, C., SEIFRIED, P. 2007, "Collaborative Spaces as Learning Environments", *3rd International ASCAAD Conference on Em'body'ing Virtual Architecture,* [Online], . Available from: http://www.ascaad.org/conference/2007/030. PDF. [April 30, 2010].

HUITT, W. 2001, "Motivation to learn: An overview", *Educational Psychology Interactive Valdosta, GA: Valdosta State University,* [Online], . Available from:

http://www.edpsycinteractive.org/topics/motivation/motivate.html. [April 30, 2010].

KIRRIEMUIR, J. 2007, "The Second Life of UK Academics", *Ariadne,* [Online], no. 53. Available from: http://www.ariadne.ac.uk/issue53/kirriemuir. [April 30, 2010].

KRAUSE, K.L., COATES, H. 2008, "Students' engagement in first-year university", *Assessment and Evaluation in Higher Education,* vol. 33, no. 5, pp. 493-505.

LAVE, J., WENGER, E. 1991, *Situated Learning - Legitimate peripheral participation,* University of Cambridge Press, Cambridge.

MEADOWS, M.T. 2008, *I, avatar - The culture and consequences of having a second life,* New Riders, Berkeley.

POWER, M. 2008. The Emergence of a Blended Online Learning Environment. *MERLOT Journal of Online Learning and Teaching [Online],* 4 (4). Available from: http://jolt.merlot.org/vol4no4/power_1208.htm. [April 30, 2010].

REUTERS, E. 2008, January 31-last update, *Poll: Most adults don't want fantasy avatars* [Homepage of secondlife.reuters.com], [Online]. Available: http://secondlife.reuters.com/stories/2008/01/31/poll-most-adults-dont-want-fantasy-avatars/ [2010, April 30] .

RYAN, M. 2001, *Narrative as Virtual Reality,* The Johns Hopkins University Press, Baltimore.

SCHEUCHER, T., BAILEY, P.H., GÜTL, C., HARWARD, V.J. 2009, "Collaborative virtual 3D environment for internet-accessible physics experiments", *REV 2009,* [Online], . Available from: http://www.iicm.tu-graz.ac.at/home/cguetl/publications/2009/Scheucher%20et%20al.%202009%20-%20REF.pdf. [April 30, 2010].

SCHMEIL, A., EPPLER, M.J. 2008, "Knowledge sharing and collaborative learning in second life: A classification of virtual 3D group interaction scripts", *Journal of Universal Computer Science,* [Online], vol. 14, no. 3. Available from: http://www.jucs.org/jucs_15_3/knowledge_sharing_and_collaborative/jucs_15_03_0665_0677_schmeil.pdf. [April 30, 2010].

SMITH, M.K. 2009, , *Communities of practice* [Homepage of The Encyclopaedia of Informal Education], [Online]. Available:

http://www.infed.org/biblio/communities_of_practice.htm [2010, April 30] .

STOVALL, I. 2003, , *Engagement and Online Learning* [Homepage of UIS Community of Practice for E-Learning], [Online]. Available: http://otel.uis.edu/copel/EngagementandOnlineLearning.ppt [2010, April 30] .

VEERMAN, A., ELSE, V.D. 2001, "Collaborative learning through computer-mediated communication in academic education ", *Paper presented at the European Perspectives on Computer Supported Collaborative Learning: Euro-CSCL, Maastricht McLuhan Institute,* .

VYGOTSKY, L.S. 1978, *Mind in Society: The Development of Higher Psychological Processes,* Harvard University Press, Cambridge, MA.

WAN, J., REDDY, M. 2009, "The self regulated community of learning within 3D virtual learning environments", [Online], . Available from: http://www.iicm.tugraz.at/home/cguetl/Conferences/ViWo/ViWo2009Workshop/finalpapers/ViWo2009Workshop_04.pdf. [October 30, 2009].

WENGER, E. 2006, , *Communities of Practice - A Brief Introduction* [Homepage of ewenger.com], [Online]. Available: http://www.ewenger.com/theory/ [2010, April 30] .

WENGER, E. 1998, , *Communities of Practice - Learning as A Social System* [Homepage of Systems Thinker], [Online]. Available: http://www.co-i-l.com/coil/knowledge-garden/cop/lss.shtml [2010, April 30] .

WIKIMEDIA 2010, May 9-last update, *Narrative* [Homepage of Wikimedia], [Online]. Available: http://en.wikipedia.org/wiki/Narrative [2010, May 9] .

YOUNG, R.M., RIEDL, M.O. 2003, "Towards an architecture for intelligent control of narrative in interactive virtual worlds", *Proceedings of the 2003 International Conference on Intelligent User Interfaces* Miami, Florida.

ZHAO, C.M., KUH, G.D. 2004, "Adding value: learning communities and student engagement", *Research in Higher Education,* [Online], vol. 45, no. 2. Available from: http://nsse.iub.edu/pdf/research_papers/Zhao_Kuh_Learning_Communities.pdf. [April 30, 2010].

University of Wales, Newport

Prifysgol Cymru, Casnewydd

Enhancing Research-Teaching Links in Higher Education
Simon K. Haslett and Hefin Rowlands (eds)
Proceedings of the Newport NEXUS Conference
Centre for Excellence in Learning and Teaching
Special Publication, No. 3, 2010, pp. 92-107
ISBN 978-1-899274-43-7

From parchment to pixels or pixels to parchment?

Julie Mathias and Tim Gillison

Department of Information Studies, Aberystwyth University, Llanbadarn Campus, Aberystwyth, Ceredigion, SY23 3DD. Email: jum@aber.ac.uk

Abstract

A knowledge of palaeography, the study of old handwriting, is essential for anyone wishing to identify, read and interpret records from earlier centuries. Palaeography is a subject offered by Aberystwyth University to campus-based, distance learning and life-long learning students following academic, vocational and non-vocational courses. This project is currently in its early stages. It seeks to use a blended-learning approach to reinforce key information previously provided to students in only written form, to clarify the link between the theory and practice of palaeography, and to enhance student engagement. This will be achieved by the creation of a collection of re-usable learning objects in a multi-media form for the benefit of a range of learners. The project consists of three inter-related parts:

1. Bite-sized video clips - the first strand involves the production of a series of short videos, each of which will concentrate on the handwriting of a specific time period. To maximise student interest and engagement with the subject, each video will focus on a local historical feature of that period and an associated record. Each video will begin with a site shot and commentary to put it in context, followed by examination and discussion of a relevant record to illustrate the key characteristics of handwriting of the time. In an attempt to increase inclusivity, two versions of each video will be produced: one which is multi-media and the other consisting of images and transcripts; the former may assist students with dyslexia, for example, and the latter those with impaired hearing.

2. Online presentations by experts in related relevant areas - the second strand of this project consists of the creation of a library of recordings of presentations by experts in related fields. Accompanying slides, illustrations, and bibliographic material are being incorporated into the learning objects, which are, again, available in multi-media and visual-only forms. This will enable off-campus students to access specialist information not normally available to them. Also, it offers students with a particular interest, further opportunities to view relevant presentations.

3. Interactive online exercises - the third strand will be a collection of interactive online exercises based upon the content of the first strand, and constructed using Wimba Create, with the objective of enabling formative self-assessment.

All these learning objects are being made available via the VLE to registered students pursuing courses in palaeography at Aberystwyth. Users of these learning objects will be canvassed in order to:

- evaluate the utility and value of the learning objects
- assess how they can be improved
- obtain views on how the project could be extended and enhanced

Future developments will be guided by this feedback.

Introduction

Palaeography and diplomatic is the study of handwriting and the structure and form of documents. It forms a key module[1] within the Department of Information Studies' (DIS) Archives Administration course,[2] taught at Aberystwyth University (AU) since 1956, and is also made available to Masters and Doctoral students following courses in related disciplines, such as English, History and Welsh. Since 2002, increasing numbers of people have opted to pursue the Archives course via distance learning.[3] These off-campus students attend three study schools in Aberystwyth. The second school is almost entirely devoted to practical work in support of the Manuscript Skills module.[4] In more recent years, with the upsurge in interest amongst the general public in family and community history, palaeography has been offered as part of the university's extra mural Certificate in Genealogical Studies, run by the School of Education and Lifelong Learning (SELL).[5] Lifelong learning students have the opportunity to follow two palaeography modules,[6] which are taught weekly at the university with visits to local archive repositories to carry out practical work.

In line with the seven foci of the DIS Learning and Teaching strategy,[7] which address the aims of the University's Learning and Teaching Strategy,[8] the purpose of this project is to enhance the learning experience of all students studying palaeography and diplomatic at AU. This will be achieved in a number of ways, which will be discussed in the project outline below.

This paper will outline the purpose of this project, discuss developments to date and the administration and findings of the pilot study, before presenting conclusions and plans for future developments.

Outline of the project

DIS at AU has offered its vocational training courses in mixed mode since setting up a specialist Open Learning Unit (OLU) in 1993. Parallel courses leading to the same qualification are offered face-to-face for campus-based students and via distance learning for people who wish to study whilst working in a relevant field. Campus-based students are able to take specialist modules developed primarily for distance learners, via open learning.[9] Distance learners attend, on

---

[1] ILM1820 Medieval and post-medieval palaeography and diplomatic

[2] Homepage of the Department of Information Studies, Aberystwyth University. Available at http://www.dil.aber.ac.uk/en/home.asp Viewed 30 April 2010.

[3] 14 campus-based students are pursuing the MScEcon in Archives Administration for the year 2009/10. The current number of students registered on the distance learning equivalent course is 137. Figure correct on 23 April 2010.

[4] DSM3810 Manuscript Skills, which is a 10 credit module concerned with post-medieval palaeography and diplomatic.

[5] Homepage of the School of Education and Lifelong Learning, Aberystwyth University. Available at http://www.aber.ac.uk/sell/ Viewed 30 April 2010.

[6] HA104 Deciphering old handwriting (10 credits) HA207: Reading historical documents in local archives (20 credits)

[7] The Department's learning and teaching priorities are based around the following foci: flexibility, innovation, collaboration, employability, reflection, equality, and staff development. Department of Information Studies. *Learning and Teaching Strategy, 2004-2009*, Aberystwyth University. February 2007, p1.

[8] These are as follows: "facilitate the enhancement of learning and teaching; improve the learning and teaching infrastructure; promote and reward excellence in learning and teaching; develop innovative new modules and programmes; develop collaborative links in the delivery of learning and teaching." Ibid, p1.

[9] Students are provided with a module pack, training by members of the OLU in time management and other essential study skills, and then work through the materials at a pace to suit their own circumstances. They can contact academic staff via the VLE with any questions they may have and they are encouraged to interact with distance learners studying the same module in order to pool ideas and offer mutual support. Assignment submission dates are pre-determined

average, three study schools and receive tuition and guidance in study skills required for this mode of learning as well as introductions to the core modules of their courses. Whereas campus-based students attend lectures, seminars and practical sessions, distance learners are supplied with their learning materials in an open learning format. Unfortunately, apart from the occasional guest speaker at a study school, the distance learners do not benefit from presentations by specialists. In an attempt to rectify this situation, for the palaeography students at least, it was decided to provide online recordings of invited speakers which could be accessed by palaeography students at an appropriate and convenient point in their studies. It is hoped a series of online presentations will be created so that current students, following courses in whatever mode, will be able to benefit from talks which are not repeated in subsequent years. Campus-based students would have the opportunity to see the presentation again at their leisure, while distance learners would be able to experience some of the sessions normally unavailable to them. Lifelong learners pursuing a course in palaeography for their own satisfaction, rather than to enhance future employment opportunities, will be given an insight into the learning experience of those enrolled on more formal vocational and academic courses. This may encourage some to pursue a similar course in the future.

A number of websites have been developed by archive services, either alone or in collaboration with academic departments within universities, which offer guidance with reading old handwriting together with interactive practical exercises of varying difficulty.[10] Efforts elsewhere to use technology to provide guidance and additional practice of transcription are apparent, although they are not necessarily made freely available to all via the web.[11] These websites are the modern equivalent of the more traditional practice of working through hard copy graded examples and checking transcripts against a master version in preparation for reading authentic documents.

Apart from providing guidance and practice in reading old handwriting, it was felt that there is further scope to make use of new methods to present information to students in a variety of forms which would help to embed it in their minds. Until now, students on the Aberystwyth palaeography courses have been supplied with handouts providing key information about the characteristic letter shapes and abbreviations associated with a particular hand of a certain period, which has been reinforced by looking at examples

---

for campus-based students, whereas distance learners set their own deadlines.

[10] For example, The National Archives, in collaboration with The School of Library, Archive and Information Studies, University College, London have developed an interactive online Palaeography Tutorial, *Palaeography: reading old handwriting 1500-1800. An online tutorial.* Available at

http://www.nationalarchives.gov.uk/palaeography / Viewed 30 April 2010. Users are given basic information on how to read and transcribe documents dated between 1500-1800 and then have the opportunity to put theory into practice with online examples of varying levels of difficulty. A joint venture between the Department of English Local History at Leicester University and the West Sussex Record Office resulted in an interactive website featuring medieval as well as early modern scripts, enhanced by an extensive bibliography of works of an academic as well as more practical nature. Department of English Local History, Leicester University. *Medieval palaeography.* Available at http://paleo.anglo-norman.org/palindex.html Viewed 30 April 2010.

[11] Academics at Leeds University created an interactive program to assist MA Renaissance Literature and PhD students learn to read C16th and C17th Secretary Hand. Digitised images of documents were incorporated into a computer program, mounted on the web, and then students' transcripts of the images could be checked against a master version which would highlight incorrectly transcribed words. Booth, A., Lindley, D. and O. Pickering. (2006). "Learning Secretary Hand: an interactive tutorial." In ed. Hanrahan, M. and D.L. Madsen. *Teaching, technology, textuality: approaches to new media.* Palgrave, 162-177.

within documents, before finally attempting to read the document as a whole.

Figure 1. Example text.

In a conversation with a campus-based dyslexic student last year, the idea of providing an audio version of the theory of palaeography handouts delivered via the VLE or podcast was mooted. The student felt that listening rather than reading would help her to absorb key information more easily. However, it is preferable to see particular letter shapes and abbreviation signs than to attempt to describe them in words. For instance, the second letter in the example (Figure 1) on the left hand side is a long forked 'r', the bar mark above the word indicates missing letters and the sign at the end which looks like the number two with a vertical stroke through it denotes a -rum ending. The word reads as 'nostrorum'.[12]

In the last year, there has been further impetus to provide alternative forms of learning due to the enrolment of someone with a hearing impairment on two of the SELL palaeography courses. It is unreasonable to expect a person to look at a document whilst lip reading or following a signer. One solution is to make a copy of the document available with the key points superimposed so that the student knows what to look for and how to interpret them.

It is clear that creating multimedia learning objects is an approach which could help to increase inclusivity of the palaeography courses and prove beneficial to all the students pursuing them. There are a number of opportunities to attend training courses within the University that offer ideas on how technology can be used to benefit learning and teaching and provide participants with the skills and technical support to turn these plans into reality. Funding is also available through the *Gwella Project* for the development of small e-learning projects and to enable staff to attend relevant workshops and conferences.[13]

Project development

Taking into account the nature of the subject, the needs of the students and currently available technology, this project has been separated into three strands, which are outlined below.

Strand 1: Bite-sized video clips

A series of short video clips will be created which will focus on the key features associated with particular forms of handwriting from the C12th to the C19th. These learning objects will provide a summary and a revision aid. Documents will be chosen which contain clear examples of classic forms of abbreviations and letter shapes associated with a particular hand and, where possible, they will be linked with the local area to heighten interest.

Identifying and selecting the right documents takes time and careful thought. Copyright will have to be obtained to use images of these records. Only then can attention be turned to providing a coherent commentary, which will both engage the attention of the listener as well as educate them. It is hoped that putting the documents

---

[12] See line 8 of example VIII, a Royal Letters Patent, 1317, Hector, LC. (1966). *The handwriting of English documents*. 2nd ed. London, Edward Arnold Publishers, 76.

[13] *Background to the Gwella Project*. Aberystwyth University. Available at: http://www.aber.ac.uk/en/is/elearning/gwella/ Viewed 30 April 2010.
Nexus. Sharing good practice in technology-enhanced learning at Aberystwyth University. Aberystwyth University. Available at: http://nexus.aber.ac.uk/xwiki/bin/view/Main/ Viewed 30 April 2010.

into context by providing a brief explanation of their purpose and incorporating images of the area in which they were created will assist in this process.

This part of the project is in an early stage of development but work has begun to identify suitable examples of documents and locations for the clips.

Strand 2: Online presentations

Strand 2, consisting of filming and processing presentations by guest speakers to make them available online to all palaeography students, is more advanced than the first strand of the project. The first such presentation was delivered by Dr Elizabeth New of the Welsh Medieval Seals Project.

Raw Material. The presentation was filmed using a Panasonic NV-GS500 mini DV video camera. The form of medium was chosen by default since that was only equipment that was available at the time. It is a good medium in many ways: relatively cheap, compact, commonly available and easily stored. However, it suffers from the disadvantage that the duration of a tape is only sixty minutes, thus entailing a pause to change tapes if the presentation exceeds this time. Whilst a tape change is quick, it does cause an interruption to the flow of the talk. The camera was capable of operating in LP (Long Play) mode, which extends tape duration to ninety minutes, but the associated reduction in quality due to the introduction of compression artefacts was unacceptable.

In order to be as unobtrusive as possible the camera was operated from the back of the room, about ten metres away from the presenter. At that distance it was still easily possible to get a close up view of the presenter; the camera is equipped with a 12x zoom (actual focal length unknown but appears to cover a range of approximately 35mm to 420mm in terms of "35mm equivalent"). Although the presenter used PowerPoint slides to accompany her talk, no attempt was made to capture them as it was understood that the PowerPoint file would be made available after the presentation.

Sound quality and clarity are important aspects of this undertaking, especially as one of the objectives is to maximise inclusivity. The aim is to capture the presenter's voice clearly and with as little interference from ambient sounds as possible. The distance between the presenter and the camera made the use of the camera's built-in microphone impractical: the quality would not be good and all extraneous sounds would be recorded in addition to the presenter's voice. Accordingly, the sound was acquired via a radio linked lapel microphone (Sony UWP-V1 kit). The camera has an input for external microphones; this is an important feature when choosing equipment for this purpose. In this instance the sound level was set to ALC (Automatic Level Control). This is the standard and "safe" option on most video cameras: the recording level of the sound is set automatically by the camera to ensure that it falls within acceptable limits: neither too loud, so that it becomes distorted, nor so low that it becomes inaudible. The level is monitored and adjusted by the camera throughout the recording. The advantage of this is that it is reliable; the disadvantage is that during the inevitable pauses in a presenter's talk, the level is automatically increased and then any extraneous, and unwanted, sounds (such as nearby computer fans, fluorescent lights humming, and so on) are faithfully recorded. The alternative is to set the level manually. This requires a sound test before the actual recording in order to establish the volume of the presenter's voice and then setting the level accordingly. If this approach went according to plan, it should dramatically decrease the intrusion of unwanted sounds. However, with this particular camera at least, although it is possible to see a display of the sound level while recording, it is not possible to adjust it without stopping the recording and then starting again. It seems that many, perhaps all, presenters are not good at anticipating how enthused and animated they will become during the course of their presentation, and how much the level of their voice will increase; thus a perhaps rather diffident sound check before the event gives a false impression of the volume to come. It might be that other cameras would permit manual adjustment during filming; this would avoid the distressing dilemma of the operator watching the sound level meter straying hopelessly off the scale and wondering whether to interrupt the recording (and the perhaps presenter) in order to rectify the problem.

As already mentioned, the presenter had undertaken to provide the PowerPoint file for our use, thus giving us access to the images which were used during the presentation. There were also a number of seals which were shown directly to the audience and not illustrated in the slides. These were photographed after the presentation using a shadowless lighting stand and a digital camera. The former proved to be a pointless refinement since the raised designs on the seals are only clearly visible when they do create shadows; the best images were obtained by using asymmetric and oblique illumination.

Processing. The video material was transferred (via Firewire) from the camera to the PC using the video editing program "Serif MoviePlus X3". It was then copied in its entirety onto a DVD. This allowed it to be watched and parsed into thematic sections based on the logical structure of the talk.

Because of the overall length of the presentation, it seemed sensible to provide the user with the option to view it in sections rather than just one long video: they may not have time to watch the whole thing in one go, or there might be sections which are either irrelevant to them, which they could avoid, or of particular interest, which they could view again.

The times of these section breaks were noted and then used in the video editing program to insert chapter markers. Each "chapter", of which there were seven, was then exported as a separate video file. The format "Windows Media Audio and Video" (*.wmv) was chosen as it provides a good compromise of file size and quality and is easily incorporated into applications.

Table 1 gives the names of the sections, their duration in minutes and their associated file sizes:

Section	Time (mins)	File size (MB)
1. Introduction	2.58	22
2. What are seals? What are they made of?	20.01	145
3. Preservation of seals	8.42	63
4. How are seals used?	19.51	144
5. Types of seals	15.33	113
6. What is shown on seals?	4.43	34
7. Recording seals	1.03	8
TOTAL	**71.31**	**529**

Table 1. Names of sections, duration and file sizes.

In addition to the video, there were the still images to be incorporated into the project; some were from the presenter's PowerPoint slides and some were photographs taken of the materials used in the presentation. It was eventually decided to use Microsoft PowerPoint to combine these resources and provide an easy way for the user to access them. A bibliography had also been provided by the presenter and this too could be included in the output.

Each section was watched again in order to produce a text transcription; this would eventually be provided for users with hearing difficulties. The transcription also contained notes and times of the use of images and objects during the presentation. This additional information was used to add the images to the appropriate slides. A text box containing an appropriate caption was grouped with each image and then timings applied to each to set the moment of their fade in and fade out.

The PowerPoint slide show begins with an opening title page. This automatically fades into a Contents page after a few seconds. The Contents page (Figure 2) has a list of section headings; each heading is in fact a link to the slide in question. Each section slide has a title, a box within which the relevant video file plays and varying numbers of still images, each with an informative caption. At the bottom of each page there is an array of four control buttons to aid navigation within the show. They are: "Contents", which goes back to the Contents page; "Previous" and "Next", which are self-explanatory; and "End", which ends the slide show. The general layout of all the slides is the same; consistency should make navigation easier for the user.

Figure 2. Contents Page.

Figure 3. Typical slide from presentation.

Figure 3 shows a typical slide from the presentation. Only one image is shown in the example; in fact there may be many images and captions on any one slide. They are all superimposed in the same place on the slide, but appear and disappear at appropriate times according to the animations applied to each image. The video is configured to start playing as soon as the page is loaded; the timings of the images are all set as offsets from the start of the video.

Once the slides had been assembled satisfactorily, the next task was to make the presentation available via the VLE. It was already appreciated that PowerPoint deals differently with video data compared with still images. The latter are incorporated into the PowerPoint file, the former remain as external files which are linked to the presentation. In some respects this is an advantage: if the video files were all contained within a monolithic file it would take a very considerable time to load and open, even over a very fast network connection; if the video files remain external to the PowerPoint file and are loaded only when required, the presentation can start much more quickly. The disadvantage is that the video files can easily become disconnected from the main file if its location, or theirs, is changed. This was a problem when mounting the presentation on the VLE: whilst there was no difficulty getting the presentation to work as far as text and images were concerned, the video was initially difficult. Despite using the "Package for CD" function in PowerPoint, which is supposed to produce a self-contained collection of files ready for distribution, collecting the output into a Zip file and then uploading that to the VLE, the reliability of the video element was poor. This may in part be a feature of our particular instance of the VLE and so is not of general interest. The solution under our circumstances was to put the video files in the web space of one of the authors and then create links to them from the PowerPoint file. This works because the location of the video files is then known and stable. On the other hand, within the VLE it seemed that the absolute location of the files would sometimes change over time; these changes seem to be known to the VLE and any links which it manages are updated accordingly but links within a file (such as our PowerPoint file) are not updated and so cease to work. The current solution is not a good one; it sufficed for piloting purposes but a more robust solution will be sought.

In keeping with the objective of increasing inclusivity, the transcript of the talk was to be made available. This would be of obvious benefit to those with hearing difficulties but may also be useful more generally. To this end, the verbatim transcript was first lightly edited to improve readability; the edited version was passed back to the presenter for approval. In fact the presenter carried out further slight editing and added a little more information for clarity. The same images as those used in the PowerPoint slides were then added to the text, using the location data already inserted into the original transcripts. This was carried out in Microsoft Word but the final product was converted (via OpenOffice's "Write" program) into a pdf file to increase accessibility. This too was mounted on the VLE, alongside the PowerPoint slide show.

This project is user-centric and thus feedback is an important element in the process; it is intended to use feedback to guide the progress of the project, both in terms of usability and content. To avoid missing an opportunity to elicit feedback from a particular group of students, the PowerPoint presentation and the transcription were made available to them on CD while the above mentioned problems with the VLE delivery route were addressed. This seemed to work well, but is not a favoured delivery route since the original agreement with the presenter was that access to the material would be restricted to registered palaeography students. Access to content via the VLE is controlled; control is lost once a CD is handed over. To at least partially address this issue, the students who were given a CD were asked to sign a form explaining its conditions of use and obliging them to either return or destroy the CD by a certain date.

Strand 3: Interactive online exercises

Interactive online exercises are being created using Wimba Create[14] to help students assess how well they have understood particular learning objects associated with the first two strands of the project.

It can be seen from the opening screen (Figure 4) how the learning object has been set out and how it should be used. In the case of the seals presentation, transcripts were used to formulate a mixture of closed and open questions, split into seven sections along the lines of the presentation itself. The quickest ones to answer are the multiple choice questions, which require the participant simply to click the correct answer and then check the answer, such as in Figure 5. Anyone clicking the wrong answer in this type of question is advised to try again.

Feedback is provided for the more challenging open questions, so that the participant is left in no doubt of the correct response and has no need to access the presentation itself to check upon the accuracy of their answer. For instance, see Figure 6. The concluding section of this learning object includes details of where to go to find further information on the subject (Figure 7).

For completeness and accuracy, the presenter of the seals talk was asked to comment on the nature of the questions posed and the answers provided. After a few minor adjustments, the questions were typed into the Wimba framework and turned into an online self assessment, which has since been mounted on the Blackboard area reserved for *Resources for Palaeography*. It will be linked to the seals presentation by being stored within the same folder.

It is proposed to ask the next cohort of campus-based and distance learning students to test the pilot version of the questions based upon the seals presentation and to request feedback on the value of this development. Modifications can be made as necessary. It is hoped that the final result will be an effective set of closed and open questions which will not only help students to gauge their understanding of a particular topic, but will help them to revise the topic

---

[14] Wimba Create is a tool with which to construct the exercises. Once created, there is no further need of Wimba. For details of potential uses of

Wimba, see
http://www.wimba.com/products/wimba_create/
Viewed 30 April 2010.

and then guide them to other sources of information on the subject.

Pilot study

As mentioned earlier, the seals presentation and transcripts were made available via the VLE and via a CD to students registered on various palaeography courses offered by the university in different modes, as well as to a small number of key staff. People were asked to view the presentation and provide feedback to assist future developments (see Appendix).

Table 2 provides details of those offered access to the learning object. The number in brackets refers to those who completed the questionnaire, which forms the Appendix. The category termed 'other' consisted of four members of AU staff and an external person, all with links to the palaeography courses.

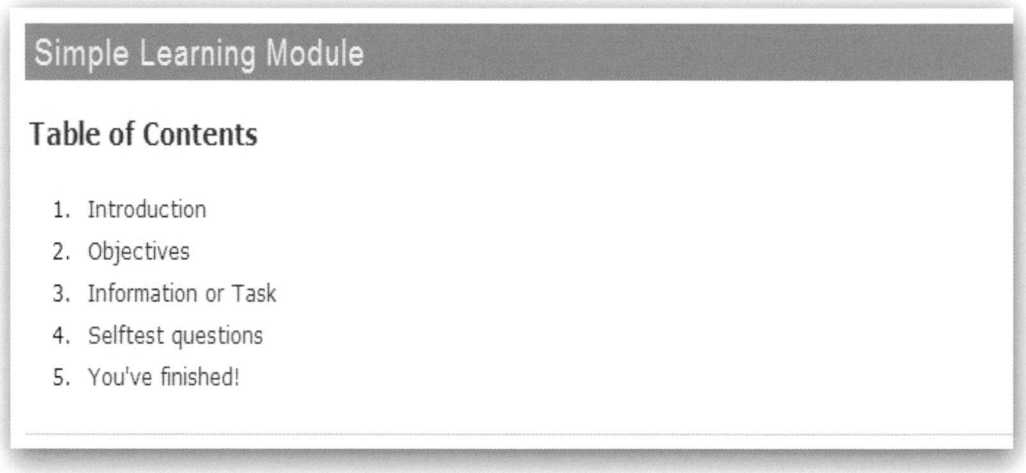

Simple Learning Module

Table of Contents

1. Introduction
2. Objectives
3. Information or Task
4. Selftest questions
5. You've finished!

Figure 4. Opening page.

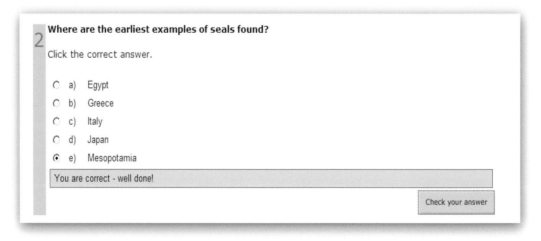

Figure 5. Example of multiple choice questions.

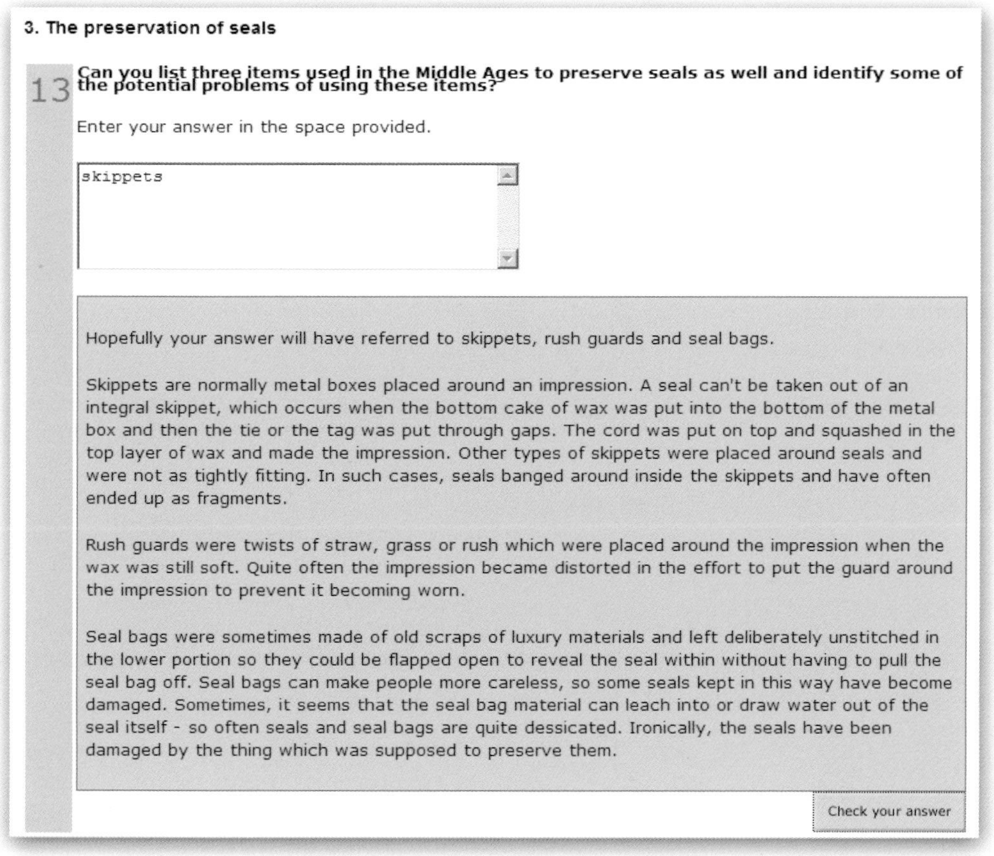

3. The preservation of seals

13 Can you list three items used in the Middle Ages to preserve seals as well and identify some of the potential problems of using these items?

Enter your answer in the space provided.

> skippets

Hopefully your answer will have referred to skippets, rush guards and seal bags.

Skippets are normally metal boxes placed around an impression. A seal can't be taken out of an integral skippet, which occurs when the bottom cake of wax was put into the bottom of the metal box and then the tie or the tag was put through gaps. The cord was put on top and squashed in the top layer of wax and made the impression. Other types of skippets were placed around seals and were not as tightly fitting. In such cases, seals banged around inside the skippets and have often ended up as fragments.

Rush guards were twists of straw, grass or rush which were placed around the impression when the wax was still soft. Quite often the impression became distorted in the effort to put the guard around the impression to prevent it becoming worn.

Seal bags were sometimes made of old scraps of luxury materials and left deliberately unstitched in the lower portion so they could be flapped open to reveal the seal within without having to pull the seal bag off. Seal bags can make people more careless, so some seals kept in this way have become damaged. Sometimes, it seems that the seal bag material can leach into or draw water out of the seal itself - so often seals and seal bags are quite dessicated. Ironically, the seals have been damaged by the thing which was supposed to preserve them.

> Check your answer

Figure 6. Example of feedback provided.

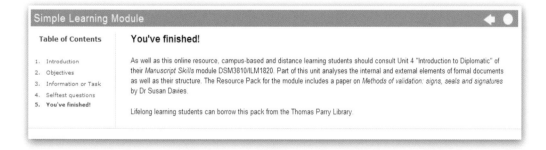

Simple Learning Module

Table of Contents

You've finished!

1. Introduction
2. Objectives
3. Information or Task
4. Selftest questions
5. You've finished!

As well as this online resource, campus-based and distance learning students should consult Unit 4 "Introduction to Diplomatic" of their *Manuscript Skills* module DSM3810/ILM1820. Part of this unit analyses the internal and external elements of formal documents as well as their structure. The Resource Pack for the module includes a paper on *Methods of validation: signs, seals and signatures* by Dr Susan Davies.

Lifelong learning students can borrow this pack from the Thomas Parry Library.

Figure 7. Final Page.

Course	Number offered access (and provided feedback)
MScEcon Archive Administration campus based	14 (3)
MScEcon Archive Administration distance learning	8 (4)
MA Medieval History campus based	2 (2)
PhD campus based	2 (1)
Genealogical Studies campus based	4 (2)
Other	5 (2)
TOTAL	**35 (14)**

Table 2. Courses with access to the learning object.

The timing of this exercise was unfortunate because the largest group given access to the learning object, campus-based students pursuing the MScEcon Archive Administration course, were completing assignments and preparing for a number of practical and theoretical examinations. However, it was decided to launch the beta version of the presentation at this time so that it would coincide with a study school which was attended by the distance learning archive students about to embark upon their palaeography module.

Five of the respondents were in their 20s, two were in their 30s, three were in their 40s, two were in their 50s and two were aged over 60.

All respondents had access to the internet: one at home via dial-up, eleven at home via broadband, nine could use the university network, and two access the internet at work. Nine of the fourteen respondents had two means of accessing the internet. One person accessed the presentation using the supplied CD and the VLE, eight used the CD only and five used the VLE only. People had different experiences when accessing the learning object, possibly due to their internet connection. On a scale 1 to 5, where 1 indicated no problem at all and 5 meant users were unable to access the presentation, five people selected 1, four chose 2, and three people each marked 3 and 4. One person did not answer this question. Those with access problems supplied further details, such as:

"the video is a bit sticky and the end of each section is not especially clear and may have broken off at some points."

"I couldn't play the CD on my Mac book so have had to play it at work. I couldn't access the presentation on Blackboard with my VPN on or off."

"the video took ages to download and then the streaming of the video was not smooth. It kept stopping which made it difficult to follow. The transcript took 6 minutes to download. In fact I had moved on to complete this questionnaire before it appeared."

"Film froze (picture still whilst commentary continuing)."

"The audio-visual was very straight forward. The power point took a little more time to access but was good once I had navigated the different links."

These comments were not entirely unexpected given the problems encountered making the video and sound work simultaneously. Increased compression of the files should reduce the time taken to download the video in future.

Six people viewed the presentation in both formats, seven selected the audio-visual version, whilst one looked at the transcripts only. Three respondents indicated that they would find the audio-visual version useful, whereas the other eleven stated that they would like access to both formats. Seven people were interested in having podcasts and ten wanted a DVD version of the presentation. One person did not state any interest in other methods of delivery. These results endorse the value of providing information in more than one format to enable students to use the format(s) most suited to their style of learning.

Although the questionnaire asked people to comment about the interest and value of each section of the presentation, for the purposes of this paper, a selection of comments about the presentation as a whole have been included to provide a flavour of the responses to this initiative:

"Dr. New's expertise and enthusiasm for what some might see as a niche area is inspiring. The whole presentation is incredibly enlightening and useful."

"Brilliant presentation-excellent images, especially pictures of damage to seals."

"I was actually at the talk Elizabeth gave so only dipped into the presentation. Excellent idea – the sound quality was correct and the picture quality was good. I was a little unsure of just watching Elizabeth's head and would have liked to have seen a few wider shots (apologies if this happens later). Brilliant idea, please let's have more!!!!! Thank you."

"Fascinating throughout."

"For a first time effort this is excellent. I look forward to more!"

"Listening to and watching the presentation on a live CD was both interesting and innovative."

Out of the ten responses to the question asking for feedback about aspects of the presentation which could be improved, three said *"none"*, one commenting further that it was a *"lovely way of learning about seals, and I had the option of rewinding [sic] and listening a second time."*

Others had useful comments, which, where practical, the developers will attempt to incorporate into an updated version. Examples include:

"I couldn't change the volume once the power point was running but you can change it if you are running it through media player."

"The files are very large and could pose problems with students who do not have high spec computers and internet access. I also would like to see sub titles which would allow deaf students to follow the presentation with ease."

"I felt it would have been better to have the text on the same time as the visual presenter."

"A time scale for each topic. A 'fast forward' option."

"Would it be possible to be able to search the sub-sections?"

A number of useful suggestions were provided for future presentations to these students, which have been noted. Final comments about the development were, on the whole, very positive and extremely encouraging. These include:

"I think this is a very useful development, particularly for distance learners. The presentation was very easy to access and I particularly liked the way that one was able to "dip" into the different sections and view them separately at leisure."

"A regular podcast would be fantastic… although would this only be available to current students? How about putting something similar into the public domain? It could get people interested and contacting the university for further information about short courses. I know I would miss not being able to access the level of knowledge that has been available to us whilst studying at Aber. Thank you."

"I thought it was excellent. The seals presentation was fascinating and I believe would be an enhancement to the students' learning experience."

"File was quite large to download especially as the only time I can download documents is in the evening when Broadband in my area runs quite slow. Overall though very good and useful project."

"Although I'm not formally studying this topic (I am just the [BSL] interpreter!) I found it extremely enjoyable and fascinating. A wonderful tool for learning. This would benefit most students – and it would be fantastic to have it also for showing examples of different hands. Ideally I feel it is better to have text and visual / film on the same document which means the same access for all, not just this version or that version."

"This is an excellent idea."

"I liked the idea of videoing presentations and then making them available to students online."

"This is a very useful and well thought out idea. The video for me is the easiest way to follow the seminars and if I do miss or do not understand something the first time around the transcribed notes of the seminar are very useful."

Conclusion and future developments

Though the project is at an early developmental stage, initial feedback from the questionnaire indicates that students are keen to have information presented to them in a number of formats and welcome this development. Distance learners benefit from presentations which they would not normally attend, campus-based students are able to revisit particular sections of talks and do not have to rely upon memory alone for information. The next phase of the project will concentrate upon gauging the efficacy of the self assessment questions based upon the seals presentation and then creating the first of a series of bite-sized palaeography clips.

An area entitled *Resources for palaeography* has been created on Blackboard, the University's VLE. The two developers of resources for this area will be able to add students following registered course in palaeography at Aberystwyth to this area, which will contain a suite of bite-sized video clips, a library of presentations and associated self assessment questions. Evaluation forms will be posted to this site so that users can provide the developers with feedback to enable the learning objects to be improved as deemed necessary.

Two more presentations provided by guest speakers have been videoed; processing the captured data will begin in the near future. In due course, consideration will be given to holding a number of focus groups, made up of students following various courses as well as staff in related fields, in order to assess the value of the new developments and gather opinions concerning future innovations.

REFERENCES

ABERYSTWYTH UNIVERSITY 2010. *Background to the Gwella Project*. Available at: http://www.aber.ac.uk/en/is/elearning/gwella/ Viewed 30 April 2010.

ABERYSTWYTH UNIVERSITY 2010. *Nexus. Sharing good practice in technology-enhanced learning at Aberystwyth University*. Available at: http://nexus.aber.ac.uk/xwiki/bin/view/Main/ Viewed 30 April 2010.

BOOTH, A., LINDLEY, D., O. PICKERING. 2006. "Learning Secretary Hand: an interactive tutorial." In ed. Hanrahan, M. and D.L. Madsen. *Teaching, technology, textuality: approaches to new media*. Palgrave, pp. 162-177.

DEPARTMENT OF ENGLISH LOCAL HISTORY, LEICESTER UNIVERSITY 2010. *Medieval palaeography*. http://paleo.anglo-norman.org/palindex.html Viewed 30 April 2010.

DEPARTMENT OF INFORMATION STUDIES, ABERYSTWYTH UNIVERSITY, 2010. *Homepage*. Available at http://www.dil.aber.ac.uk/en/home.asp Viewed 30 April 2010.

DEPARTMENT OF INFORMATION STUDIES, 2007. *Learning and Teaching Strategy, 2004-2009*, Aberystwyth University.

HECTOR, L. C. 1966. *The handwriting of English documents* (2nd ed). London, Edward Arnold Publishers.

SCHOOL OF EDUCATION AND LIFELONG LEARNING 2010. *Aberystwyth University Homepage*. Available at http://www.aber.ac.uk/sell/ Viewed 30 April 2010.

THE NATIONAL ARCHIVES 2010. *Palaeography: reading old handwriting 1500-1800. An online tutorial*. Available at http://www.nationalarchives.gov.uk/palaeography/ Viewed 30 April 2010.

APPENDIX: Evaluation of the presentation about seals

The presentation about seals is the first in a series of multi-media resources designed to complement and enhance your learning experience. It would be very helpful if you could answer the following questionnaire to enable us to evaluate the resource and to guide future developments. All responses will be anonymised. This should take no more than 10 minutes of your time.

A. About you

1. Are you:
- male ☐
- female ☐

2. Please indicate your age:
- under 30 ☐
- 30-39 ☐
- 40-49 ☐
- 50-59 ☐
- 60+ ☐

3. Which course you are following?
- MSc Econ Archives Administration ☐
- MA History ☐
- Genealogical Studies ☐
- Other – please state ....

4. Are you following your course:
- On campus ☐
- Via distance learning ☐

5. What sort of access do you have to the internet? Tick all that apply:
- None ☐
- Home: Dial-up ☐
- Home: Broadband ☐
- University network ☐
- Work network ☐
- Other – please state ....

B. Access

6. How did you access this presentation?
- Moodle ☐
- Blackboard ☐
- Other – please state ....

7. How easy did you find it to access the presentation, where 1= no problem at all and 5= unable to access. Please circle:

    1   2   3   4   5

Please state any problems encountered ....

8. Which format did you use?
- Audio-visual (i.e. sound and images) ☐
- Visual only (i.e. text and images) ☐
- Both formats ☐

9. Which format(s) would be useful to you?
- Audio-visual (i.e. sound and images) ☐
- Visual only (i.e. text and images) ☐
- Both formats ☐

10. Would you be interested in other methods of delivery, such as :
- Podcast ☐
- DVD ☐
- Other – please state ....

C. Use

11. In Table 3, please
- indicate which sections of the presentation you have viewed and on how many occasions. If you viewed a section more than once, please indicate why in the comments section
- rate each section of the presentation and the presentation as a whole for interest, where 1=very interesting and 5= not interesting at all;
- rate each section of the presentation and the presentation as a whole for value to your studies, where 1=invaluable and 5=irrelevant.

Section	No. of times viewed	Interest	Value	Comments
1. Introduction				
2. What are seals?				
3. Preservation of seals				
4. How seals are used				
5. Types of seals				
6. What is shown				
7. Recording seals				
8. Bibliography				
Whole presentation				

Table 3. Survey grid.

D. Improvements and developments

12. Please state any aspects of the presentation which, in your opinion, could be improved.

....

13. How could this be achieved?

....

14. Please indicate any other topics which you think would make useful / interesting presentations.

....

15. Do you have any other comments about this development?

....

Thank you for taking the time to complete this questionnaire. Your help is much appreciated.

University of Wales, Newport

Prifysgol Cymru, Casnewydd

Enhancing Research-Teaching Links in Higher Education
Simon K. Haslett and Hefin Rowlands (eds)
Proceedings of the Newport NEXUS Conference
Centre for Excellence in Learning and Teaching
Special Publication, No. 3, 2010, pp. 108-131
ISBN 978-1-899274-43-7

ABSTRACTS

This chapter presents abstracts of other papers presented at the *Newport NEXUS Conference 2010* for which a full written paper is not available. The abstracts are organised by symposium.

SYMPOSIUM - FLEXIBLE LEARNING IN EMPLOYMENT AND COMMUNITY SCENARIOS

Work-based learning in the Heads of the Valleys.

Kelly Edwards and Kirsten Merrill-Glover

Centre for Community & Lifelong Learning, Innovation Centre Ebbw Vale NP23 8XA. Email: Kelly.Edwards@newport.ac.uk; Kirsten.Merrill-Glover@newport.ac.uk

The National Assembly for Wales Enterprise and Learning Committee holds that Welsh universities have a pivotal role to play in managing the economic downturn and providing long term plans to facilitate a more skilled and educated workforce. The notion of 'Lifelong Learning' has been revived based on the presumption that economic competiveness and future prosperity require a deepening of the workforce's skills base. A recent report from the Committee recommends that the Welsh Assembly Government "should view higher education as an economic development tool' (National Assembly for Wales, Enterprise and Learning Committee, October 2009).

Wales continues to have comparatively high numbers of individuals in the workforce who have little or no qualifications (UCU,2009). The promotion of lifelong learning as manifested in 'Work-based learning' initiatives is seen as a route to up-skilling individuals in the workplace on the presumption that this will be of benefit to the individual, the economy and society. Confirming the role of higher education in the planned up-skilling of the workforce through work-based learning, the Welsh Assembly Government recently announced a multi-million pound investment in a collaboration between the University of Wales, Newport and Glamorgan University namely, the Universities Heads of the Valleys Institute (UHOVI). UHOVI will offer community-based higher education opportunities with a primary focus on employability and vocational qualifications.

This paper describes the development of work-based learning (WBL) provision in the Heads of the Valleys region from within the University of Wales, Newport Centre for Community and Lifelong Learning. Based in Tredegar, Bleanau Gwent and reaching out to non-traditional learners within the workplace, the provision aims to raise skills levels and promote lifelong learning amongst work-based adults in an area which is characterised by social and economic disadvantage.

Since its implementation in 2007, over 250 work-based learners from over 90 different organisations have engaged with the WBL programme studying ten credit modules at level 4 that are drawn from the Certificate of HE in (Combined Open Studies). In consultation with Newport Business School the project has developed a business and IT curriculum in response to employer/employee demand. Contingent upon demand, courses are delivered within the workplace and at community venues within easy access for work-based participants.

This paper is based on the experiences of engaging with employers and employees with traditionally low participation rates at HE level. It considers the lessons thus far learned and identifies the challenges associated with engaging people in employment who have little or no prior experiences of higher education study and the extent to which an instrumental curriculum can and does contribute to education as a tool for social justice.

Skills for employment in the 21st century.

Ian Evans

Newport Business School, University of Wales, Newport, Lodge Road, Caerleon, South Wales, NP18 3QT. Email: Ian.Evans@newport.ac.uk

In its strategy document, *Skills That Work for Wales: A Skills and Employment Strategy and Action Plan,* the Welsh Assembly Government states:

"A highly-skilled workforce is essential for an innovative knowledge economy, and we need a competitive, sustainable higher education (HE) sector to produce high-level skills. The policy landscape has changed since Reaching Higher, our strategy for HE in Wales, was published in 2002. Now is the time to refresh our agenda, to ensure that the sector can respond to the challenge of delivering our ambitious goals for skills and employment." (Source: *Skills That Work for Wales: A Skills and Employment Strategy and Action Plan,* Welsh Assembly Government Publication, p. 6)

It is a widely held belief that our formal education system and the organisations within it (i.e. Schools, FE Colleges and HE Institutions) have the responsibility of providing the necessary skills to produce the knowledge economy.

The knowledge or skills gap in our society (whether it is real or perceived) is seen by employers as a barrier to achieving sustained growth in profitability. However, do our educational organisations live up to their responsibility of preparing learners for the world of work in the 21st century?

The work place has evolved at a tremendous pace over the last twenty years. This evolution has occurred not only via the emergence of greater technology but also in the growth of expectations placed upon employees by their employers. The expectation is that employees 'hit the ground running' and I believe there is a distinct lack of patience displayed by employers in allowing their staff to grow into, an initially, unfamiliar role.

Given the rate at which the work place has changed in recent times, the following question is relevant: Have our educational organisations (particularly FE and HE) evolved at the same rate as the work place over the last twenty years in terms of providing relevant qualifications?

Seeing as many employers are of the mind that many new employees do not have the appropriate skills then it begs the question as to whether or not FE and HE institutions are providing the skills required for the modern work place. Some employers feel that even basic skills are not being properly taught in our educational institutions, let alone the higher level skills required for building a successful knowledge economy.

Finally, if it is perceived that our educational organisation are not providing the relevant skills for a modern workforce, then what must be done to ensure that the expectations of employers are met in terms of provision of more relevant qualifications? This presentation will provide an introduction to research focusing on two questions:

1. What are the relevant skills required to build a successful knowledge economy?
2. To what extent do modern educational organisations provide these skills?

E-working, agile working practices and training needs in the public sector in Wales.

Margaret Davies

Equinex Research & Development Unit, Centre for Community & Lifelong Learning, University of Wales, Newport, Lodge Road, Caerleon, South Wales, NP18 3QT. Email: Margaret.Davies2@newport.ac.uk

This study examined the process of implementing agile working in two local authorities in Wales with the intention of gathering best practice and developing training for managers and employees.

Purpose. To explore the need for training amongst employees and managers in two local authorities in South East Wales following previous research into the training needs of managers and employees in Wales/UK which had identified core training requirements from a number of organisations. To identify training requirements and develop training opportunities for the public sector in the area of e-working, teleworking, agile working. These to be piloted and evaluated using feedback from managers and employees.

Approach. A series of meetings was held with representatives of various working groups looking to introduce new working practices into two local authorities. The intention was to compare the needs for training support for managers and employees implementing agile/flexible working practices in the public sector with the findings from previous research relating to the core training needs of managers and employees of a variety of organisations in Wales/UK. Training packages were devised to be piloted and evaluated using feedback from managers and staff about the processes of implementation of this new way of working.

Findings. The research found a strong match between the core needs identified by previous research and the needs indicated from the discussions with the working groups. However, the research also found significant differences in the practices of implementation of this new way of working between the two authorities, which had implications for the types of training support required by employees and managers. For example, there were differences in the "offer" made to employees to support changes in working practices which may have implications for employee motivation; the language used in policy development was different in the two local authorities. There were indications that some managers would have more difficulty than others in managing the process; the "freelance" issue of workers who are "too" independent was a concern among some managers. The work-life balance issue and the effect on motivation appeared different for different employees.

Organisations and staff have to adapt themselves to and master different methods, procedures, tools, techniques, labour and human relations, etc., in order to effectively implement this new way of working. Training for staff and managers needs to reflect this.

Research implications. A longitudinal study of this implementation in two local authorities would provide useful information to support models for the public sector in Wales and UK.

Research the push-pull factor in this new way of working (Is it a choice or is it imposed?).

Following findings indicating that some employees live considerable distances from the local authority, living overseas in one case, an examination of the effect of agile working (where the worker lives a considerable distance from the employer) on employee motivation and commitment to the organisation may provide useful insights.

What does "retention" mean to students participating in part-time community based Higher Education.

Ceri Jones and Annettte Roche

Community University of the Valleys –East, Centre for Community & Lifelong Learning, University of Wales, Newport, 11 Gwent Shopping Centre, Tredegar, NP22 3EJ, Wales. Email: Ceri.Jones6@newport.ac.uk; Annette.Roche@newport.ac.uk

In 2006 Liz Thomas argued that: To improve student retention and success in the context of widening participation there is a need to listen to students' voices and use this to inform policy and practice (Liz Thomas 2006,2)

This laudable aim is not however the norm, as most policy and practice in relation to retention is informed by data collection methods that narrowly define success in terms of how many "Bums on Seats" (Liz Thomas 2000) are retained and, by extension, how many students complete their chosen course of study. These methods have a resonance and relevance in relation to all forms of provision but when applied to part-time community based provision certain contradictions become apparent.

It is difficult to use the classic academic definition of retention in relation to the students participating in community based higher education for example, simply because many don't initially see completing a linear programme of study as a benchmark of achievement or in some cases, as being overly important. The roll on-roll off nature of the provision allied to a fairly diverse and changing curriculum lends itself to individuals defining their own learning journeys, which means they are, in essence, shaped by the needs, aspirations and circumstances of the individual and not directly fashioned to reflect pathways of continuation that meet the needs of the institution. That said, most students do eventually accept the institutional view, but in their formative exploration of both themselves and how they fit into the realm of academia formal measures of retention are seen by some to be at best cursory and at worst irrelevant. As a provider of community based higher education this creates an inherent dichotomy, in the sense that we sit in the middle of two contradictory forces: we have to accept the institutional view of retention and provide detailed retention data, while working with students who are initially not overly concerned with linear forms of academic retention.

The evidence in the body of the presentation taken from two on-going research projects suggests that students, in various ways, define retention in relation to what factors keep them coming back. To extend the journey metaphor, many of the group through circumstance or design, have made significant diversions along the way: the only constant is the fact that all have managed to find ways to continue their journey.

To insert a caveat at this point, the groups in question have all managed to find ways to balance the external forces that impact on their trek through the academic foothills. We are fully aware however, of the fact that for some, the journey, for a myriad of reasons, has taken a different course or become stalled in the face of seemingly impassable barriers.

That said, If we act on Liz Thomas' suggestion and actually listen to our students, how do they define their academic journeys and by extension how could we use this information to inform policy and practice?

Learning through research: undergraduate projects amongst the Jewish community in Cardiff.

Nick Swann

Newport School of Education, University of Wales, Newport, Lodge Road, Caerleon, South Wales, NP18 3QT.

The second year of the Religious Studies BA programme at University of Wales, Newport is developing a strong interpersonal research strand. Two new 'short, fat' modules work together for this: 'Anthropology and Religion' and 'Research in Religion and Culture' ('RRC'), the former supplying the basic theory and methods for conducting the latter. Based on this student-led research, the RS programme aims to build up a record of faith groups in South Wales.

In spring 2009, at the suggestion of Beacon for Wales, the Chair of the Cardiff Reform Synagogue approached the Religious Studies team at University of Wales, Newport asking if we could help document Cardiff's dwindling Jewish Community. This chimed well the team's plans, and we were happy to oblige. Although in the long-term the project may involve members of staff conducting research, initially four second year students are to carry out research projects negotiated with the synagogue and supervisory academic staff. Student outputs from these projects may include MP3 files contributing to an audio tour of Jewish Cardiff; literature for the synagogue; and web page content as well as perhaps the more traditional project write-up. This paper looks at the experiences of these students, and the pedagogic effects of introducing independent (albeit well-supported) research at a relatively early stage in their degree programme.

Foundation degrees: working collaboratively to create a bridge between work-based learning and academic learning in higher education.

Caroline McLachlan[1], Kathryn Sweet[2] and Sara Scott[3]

[1]Newport School of Education, University of Wales, Newport, Lodge Road, Caerleon, South Wales, NP18 3QT. Email: caroline.mclachlan@newport.ac.uk

[2]Bridgend College, Cowbridge Road, Bridgend, CF31 3DF.

[3]Coleg Menai, Ffriddoedd Road, Bangor LL57 2TP

Foundation Degrees are work-related higher education qualifications, which have been introduced by universities and higher education institutions to help adults to equip themselves with high-level skills that employers are looking for. They have been designed with help from industry and combine academic learning with work-based training. [Welsh Assembly Government Foundation Degrees_.htm]

The session will be a workshop which will explore the processes and procedures which the University of Wales Newport and five of the partner colleges (CPI.s) have developed collaboratively to deliver Foundation Degrees in Early Years Care & Education, Learning Support, Secondary/ Post-16 and Learning Support Primary. It will explore with the audience some of the tensions in creating an interface between work-based learning and academic learning and in ensuring that there is parity of learning experience for students who are studying at institutions in five different geographical areas. There will be an opportunity to evaluate the range of documentation which provides a clear framework for students and enables them to apply theoretical frameworks, which are an integral element of module delivery, to their individual practice.

Examples of Reflective Practice Logs will be shared at the workshop, together with details of other assessment practices which also contribute to collaborative and cooperative working, these include the negotiating of assignments and the strengths and complexities of blind cross-college marking for sample assignments from all modules. These complexities are exacerbated for one student cohort at a college in North Wales who work bilingually through the medium of Welsh and English. Many of these students speak Welsh as their first language are more comfortable with module discussions in Welsh and yet choose to write assignments in English as the availability of appropriate reading materials at HE level is limited.

A small part of the session will be delivered bilingually to enable workshop participants to experience this aspect of our collaborative provision.

UHOVI: a university initiative for regeneration.

Chris O'Malley

Pro Vice-Chancellor's Office, Regional and International Development, University of Wales, Newport, Lodge Road, Caerleon, South Wales, NP18 3QT. Email: chris.o'malley@newport.ac.uk

The University of Wales, Newport is working in partnership with the University of Glamorgan in developing a new body called the Universities Heads of the Valleys Institute (UHOVI). This initiative is being designed to be a catalyst for transformation of the Heads of the Valleys region, which has for many decades been suffering the effects of de-industrialisation, loss of traditional employment, a weak skills profile, poor health levels and low income and aspirations.

The UHOVI initiative has been based on the premise that successful regeneration of communities cannot be achieved solely through physical construction programmes and incentives to investors – it needs to begin with the people themselves, their skills, aspirations, attitudes and relationships to each other and the rest of the world.

DCELLS has agreed to support the Business Plan that the two Universities have submitted to them for UHOVI. This plan sets a target of reaching 4,070 FTE student places in the region by 21013-14, and a total annual turnover for UHOVI in excess of £20m. Funding has also been obtained for four ESF-funded programmes, with a projected total value in the Heads of the Valleys of up to £15m. These include a programme of Foundation Degrees and another in Work-Based Learning.

In order to succeed in the regeneration and transformation objective, it has been accepted by all stakeholders that UHOVI cannot simply represent business as usual for the universities, with academic programmes being developed and delivered in the same way as normal. Partnership structures have been set up that involve the universities carrying out collaborative planning with each other, with the four regional FE Colleges, the Local Education Authorities, employers, schools, community groups and other stakeholders. It involves not only an integrated curriculum offering being jointly marketed, but also joint academic infrastructure to provide a coherent offering to the student.

A consultation exercise is being organised that looks, not simply at whether a given programme is of potential interest to employers and potential students, but at what the major strategic issues and opportunities are for the region across a number of key sectors, and how educational intervention can make a decisive difference to these.

The timescales for carrying out this form of consultation and collaborative planning do not sit easily alongside the deadlines for submissions to the ESF-funded programmes that provide a significant part of the funding for the initiative, so this tension has to be managed.

A further dimension to this work is the action research being undertaken in the Heads of the Valleys on pedagogical innovation possibilities by David Egan of UWIC, commissioned by the Heads of the Valleys partnership, and a panel of educational experts with whom he will be working to draw up recommendations for new initiatives to develop more effective ways of promoting and delivering learning in the region at a number of levels.

Interim conclusions from both this work and consultation with sector experts and employers will be presented at the NEXUS conference in June.

Rethinking teaching in Higher Education.

Cynthia Weston

McGill University, Department of Educational and Counselling Psychology, Teaching and Learning Services. McLennan Library, 3459 McTavish Street, Montreal, Quebec H3A 1Y1, Canada.

As university professors, we are usually hired for disciplinary expertise, and often feel unprepared for the complexities of our teaching role. Given this situation, it is not uncommon to teach in ways that are intuitive, familiar and comfortable. However, this sometimes does not lead to the kind of deep learning for students that we hope to achieve. In this session we will examine how an intentional approach to course design and teaching can be a catalyst for deep learning for students.

A paradigm shift is occurring in higher education - from information transmission approaches to teaching which focus on covering content, towards learning centered approaches to teaching which focus on facilitating students' construction of knowledge (e.g., Ramsden, 1992; Kember & Kwan, 2002). This shift is occurring, in part, because we know more about how students learn and more about how our approaches to teaching influence students' approaches to learning (e.g. Biggs, 2003; Entwistle, 2000; Trigwell, Prosser & Waterhouse, 1999). When information transmission approaches to teaching are used, students tend to adopt surface approaches to learning, such as memorizing information for an exam which results in short term retention of content. When learning centered approaches to teaching are used, students tend to adopt deeper approaches to learning in which they seek to understand content and link it to their previous experience; this results in learning that is longer lasting. Deep learning is among the most fundamental goals of higher education.

How can we design courses that are more learning centered; that focus on deeper learning? We will consider factors that contribute to deep learning, such as level of academic challenge and students' active engagement with the content (Kinzie,2010; NSSE, 2008). We will then consider how these factors can be concretely translated into our teaching. The Course Design and Teaching Workshop (Saroyan and Amundsen, 2004), initially developed at McGill University in 1993 and now adapted in various forms at numerous universities nationally and internationally, has integrated factors associated with deep learning into a learning centered approach to teaching. The course design process guides instructors through a cycle of intentional decisions about course components (content, learning outcomes, instructional strategies, and assessment). These components must be tightly and continuously aligned to achieve the desired student learning (e.g., Entwistle,2010). This process has worked because of the commitment of individual professors who invest time in enhancing their teaching through a process of intentional decisions, practice, peer learning and feedback, and personal reflection. Although challenging and sometimes uncomfortable, at McGill the process has been transformational – for teaching and for student learning.

SYMPOSIUM - TECHNOLOGY ENHANCED LEARNING

Putting the play in plagiarism: making games as assessment for learning.

Mike Reddy

Newport Business School, University of Wales, Newport, Lodge Road, Caerleon, South Wales, NP18 3QT. Email: mike.ready@newport.ac.uk

In an evolving age, where Music has never seen so much growth but the traditional Music Industry has been struggling to adapt, the value of ownership of Intellectual Property (IP) has been called into question. Similar post-modern discussion of the emphasis on provenance of academic information, rather than its application, has challenged conceptions of higher education. The 4Rs of Higher Education have evolved from practical workshops on the future of HE facilitated by the author:

1. RIGHTS - Lecturer Rights are often not recognised or considered, while Student Rights are.
2. RESPONSIBILITIES - Similarly for Student Responsibilities (and for later experiences, Student Expectations in a commercialised education sector).
3. REFLECTION - Under-represented for both staff and students, but the latter case is not surprising - mostly students just get to fill out a module feedback questionnaire and even the NSS stuff isn't particularly good at setting the student's own position in the educational .
4. RISK - The biggest surprise was that both academic colleagues and students involved said not enough risk was being taken, and institutional reaction to risk was to inhibit it.

Consequences of using the 4Rs for plagiarism prevention require some "de-comfort zoning" of academics, as well as building awareness of traditional academic processes by students and school teachers. "Putting the 'play' in Plagiarism" is a workshop in creating a board game. It is based on a business training workshop that evolved out 'Sandpitting' to visualise current state and future obstacles/opportunities. It is based on the concept of 'Paizogogy'; the learning by collaborating to make games, although video or performance can be substituted. The workshop consists of several stages:

1. The Problem Identification Game - where participants reflect on their own game playing, before addressing the (multiple or pre-set) issues.
2. the 15 minute game challenge - where participants have paper, pens and card and 15 minutes to make a prototype game. NOTE: No-one has ever failed to make a game in the quarter hour!
3. the supervised playthrough - Groups of 2-5 (ideally 3) work through the games of each of them, with a short break or two
4. Identifying common themes - similar issues, games or experiences are banded together
5. OPTIONAL Extra elements to be done on trust at a distance or, less likely, at a second session.
6. silent play through of selected games - some of the games are played without the intervention of the designer, which highlights assumptions, confusions and obstacles to presenting the idea
7. blind play through of selected games - games are played without the participation at all of the designer, again to highlight assumptions, confusions and obstacles to presenting the idea
8. participants are brought back together again. Potential for homework to create second game, up to as great a level of polish as is possible.

The main aim of the workshop is to clarify and abstract the elements of the issues facing participants, many of which are merely about pattern recognition and, more importantly, debate/discussion/dissemination of the problem itself. As applied to plagiarism prevention, discussion to raise issues of learning and assessment are overlaid onto the practical workshop, rather than participant's own research/educational needs.

An investigation into the rights and entitlements learning journeys and skills development impact experienced by 14 to 19 year olds when utilising the Futurelab Greater Expectation project's InfoCow Web 2.0 innovation resource.

Matt Chilcott[1], Kieron Kirkland[2] and Ina Pruegel[1]

[1]Institute of Digital Learning, University of Wales, Newport, Allt-yr-yn Campus, Allt-yr-yn Avenue, Newport, NP20 5DA, United Kingdom. Email: Matthew.Chilcott@newport.ac.uk; ina.prugel@newport.ac.uk

[2]Futurelab.

The Futurelab led Greater Expectations project has developed a web portal site 'InfoCow', designed to provide impartial advice to 14 to 19 year olds about their rights and entitlements as young people. It offers inspirational digital media alongside user generated content to empower young people in making informed decisions about their lives. In so doing the InfoCow web portal provides digital approaches to address barriers and widen access to social and educational opportunities and serves as a mechanism of supporting life skills decision making and promoting well being for young people.

These objectives support a number of initiatives within education and children's services, including Becta's Harnessing Technology focus on developing 'demand-led' reform and confident use of technology that closes the gap for disadvantaged learners, the Children's Plan, and increasing learner voice and personalised learning.

The recent Pupil and Parent guarantee's draft legislation highlights that young people's awareness of their rights and entitlements continues to be a priority. For these demand-led, personalised agendas to be effective, a better understanding of learners' own interests, methods of engagement and use of digital media to achieve their aspirations and entitlements must be pursued.

This study evaluates young people's access and engagement with online sites and media content. It gives insights into online participation and connections as well as content preferences, identifying what attracts users to access sites and engage with topics and different media to better address engagement strategies, networked environments and media content for accessibility and empowerment. Qualitative evidence has highlighted factors that impact on young people's motivation to engaging in finding out more about their rights. It has been identified that there is an apparent 'catch 22' in that frequently young people were only motivated to find out more when they felt these rights have been contravened. However, without the existing knowledge of their rights and entitlements, they were unsure when this was.

Significant numbers of young people engage with online media both as part of their recreational activities as well as part of their education or work lives, using a wide range of different types of media online, including video, mini games, and diverse social networking activities. There is a role for digital technology and online media in supporting young people to engage in information about their rights and entitlements.

Young people access a diverse range of information through individual choice. The Infocow site provides a platform to accommodate flexibility and individual choice. As such it offers enough information sources to cater for individual needs and offers potential routes to connect young people with the knowledge and networks to support them to engage with their rights.

These findings highlight the need for skills in empowerment for young people alongside the opportunity for future evaluation into the application of traditional and digital 'outlets' for young people to utilise their rights and entitlements.

All's fair in love, war and student evaluation of teaching effectiveness!: exploratory case studies from two UK universities.

Joanna Jones[1], Ruth Gaffney-Rhys[1], Edward Jones[1] and Alan Hayes[2]

[1]Newport Business School, University of Wales, Newport, Allt-yr-yn Campus, Allt-yr-yn Avenue,

Newport, NP20 5DA, United Kingdom. Email: jo.jones@newport.ac.uk

[2]University of Bath

In Higher Education Institutions (HEIs) throughout the world, students are asked to complete module evaluation surveys. It could be argued that, in UK HEIs, these evaluations have tended to form part of wider quality assurance processes, with emphasis upon student satisfaction. Whereas in other countries, such as the US and Australia, the emphasis has been placed upon rating of teaching effectiveness with a view to influencing pay, promotion and tenure. (Nullty 2008; Dommeyer et al 2004). Due to the prevalence and importance of student evaluation of teaching effectiveness (SETE) surveys, it is unsurprising that many academics have researched this area. However, as early as 1984, Marsh identified that there were marked differences in opinion regarding the usefulness, reliability and validity of such surveys. The move to online surveys has further complicated the debate. It is no longer unusual for surveys to be administered via an online environment (Donovan et al 2007). Disadvantages relating to online surveys are now being documented, for example, lower response rates (Nulty 2008; Dommeyer et al 2004) and students experiencing technical difficulties (Andersen et al 2005). Additionally, a recent US study (Barkhi & Williams, 2009) discussed the impact of electronic media on faculty evaluation. Analysis focussed upon the mean scores (not any extended / freeform comments) and revealed that students were more likely to express extreme responses to scale questions in the electronic environment. Many researchers (e.g. Shelvin et al 2000; Pounder 2007) have questioned the fairness of module surveys and Crumbley and Reichelt (2009) raised concerns relating to defamation. Just as the Barkhi & Williams (2009) study identified that students are more likely to express extreme scale scores in an online survey, this study has assessed if students are also more likely to make extreme comments in an online survey.

This paper disseminates research completed within the context of two UK universities, one predominantly viewed as a teaching institution, the other being traditionally research-lead. The context of the research relates to the potential reassessment of SETE surveys in the UK, linked to the possible change in government and the reduction in sector funding; and equally the move to online completion of module surveys. The research identifies how module surveys are currently utilised within the case study institutions and assesses if this is likely to change in the future. The impact that online survey methods may have on students' extended / freeform responses is evaluated and the weight that decision-makers give to extended comments is assessed. Finally, the need for HEIs to protect themselves from legal proceedings as a result of defamation, linked to module surveys, is also considered. The study was administered utilising student questionnaire, semi-structured interviews with academics and management / administrators and the review of policy documentation. Findings are rich and varied and include evidence that students are more likely to make extreme comments in an online environment. It documents significant disquiet amongst academics regarding a possible move to more overtly linking SETE surveys to promotion and tenure decisions. Additionally, a clear misunderstanding regarding defamation pervaded both institutions.

Digital Repository – Launch.

Lesley May

Learning and Information Services, Library Services, University of Wales, Newport, Lodge Road, Caerleon, South Wales, NP18 3QT

The UWN repository was set up in 2008, as part of the Welsh Repository Network, a JISC funded project. Find it at http://repository.newport.ac.uk. As of March 2010 it holds 200 unique metadata records, of which 31 are full text items. In order for our research to have international visibility, research active staff need to be encouraged to deposit their research in the repository, either via self deposit or via mediated deposit. Launching the Repository at the Nexus Conference would allow Repository and research active staff to showcase the digital repository and promote its use by staff at the University. Additionally it would offer an ideal time to demonstrate the functionality of the resource/answer questions and offer brief training on self deposit.

Or Equivalent: digital video as an alternative to the written essay assignment.

David Longman and Lynne Jones

Newport School of Education, University of Wales, Newport, Lodge Road, Caerleon, South Wales, NP18 3QT. Email: david.longman@newport.ac.uk, lynne.jones@newport.ac.uk

"Or Equivalent" comes from fairly common standard wording used in most assessment descriptors in course handbooks and validation documents, particularly where the assessment task is a written paper. Along with a prescribed number of contact hours and independent study hours validated courses will often include such assessment rubrics as "A 2500 essay on an assigned topic, or equivalent".

This presentation describes and discusses workshops with teacher training students in which they are asked to create a short 1-3 minute video for use in a classroom setting. The video is required to have a key teaching point or learning outcome aimed at Key Stage 2 or Early Years children.

This presentation therefore concludes with a discussion about the potential of a digital video as an assessment product that might satisfy the notion of 'or equivalent' We hope to show that making a video can meet the requirements not only of learning outcomes but also of assessment criteria.

Student diversity in the development of digital literacies.

Nicola Woods[1] and Simon Phillips[2]

[1]Newport School of Education, University of Wales, Newport, Lodge Road, Caerleon, South Wales, NP18 3QT. Email: Nicola.woods@newport.ac.uk

[2] Student Services, University of Wales, Newport, Lodge Road, Caerleon, South Wales, NP18 3QT. Email: Simon.Phillips1@newport.ac.uk

Responding to shifting student demographics and the perceived challenge of diversity, universities have sought ways to adapt pedagogical policies to a new student population. However, few of these initiatives genuinely engage with the shift from elite to mass provision. In particular, it appears that pedagogical approaches in HE tend to underestimate the value and importance both of what students already know and of the diverse approaches that they take to learning (MacKinnon and Manathunga 2003). The question of how students use their knowledge to develop digital competencies is crucial in the modern 'digital age' (Kennedy *et al* 2008)

Using an ethnographic approach, the research presented in this paper explores the ways of learning that students adopt to develop digital literacies, and also provides insights into the wider context of students' experiences and expectations of technology. Over 50 students enrolled on a range of undergraduate programmes participated in the study: men and women of different ages (18-58 years), diverse cultural backgrounds and various walks of life. How do these students develop digital literacies? How do they use their technological skills to support other aspects of learning (e.g. discipline-specific learning)? How do they use digital tools in work and in leisure? How does technology impact on social life and family relationships? These are some of the questions that students themselves have raised and discussed in focus group conversations about their experiences with digital media. The presentation draws on audio recordings, photographic evidence and video diaries produced by student participants.

Discussion focuses on student narratives about the development of digital literacies: students report a lack of confidence in traditional methods of teaching and comment on their own diverse learning approaches, in which play, collaborative recreation and risk taking are often noted as key strategies. Students reveal the wide variety of resources and sources of support they draw on to assist their learning and also discuss perceived obstacles and barriers to developing digital skills. Listening to students' experiences leads us to question the value of generalised and simplified categories that have been proposed for explaining learners' levels of digital competence (such as 'digital native' and 'digital immigrant' (Prensky 2001), for example).

Drawing on students' expressed views, we argue that in order to best support the development of digital competencies, it is necessary to both recognise the multiple literacies that students bring with them to university and appreciate the ways of learning that students pursue in the wider social and cultural context of their experience: e.g. within family and friendship groups, in work situations and in recreational contexts.

Case study on the use of Moodle to increase student participation in formative assessment.

Rosemary Eaton

Newport Business School, Newport Business School, University of Wales, Newport, Lodge Road, Caerleon, South Wales, NP18 3QT. Email: rosemary.eaton@newport.ac.uk

One of the areas in which I currently teach is assessed by an externally set computer based assessment (CBA). It has been recognised that there has been considerable apathy displayed by students in the past in relation to participating in the formative assessments that have been offered. Excuses given range from 'I was not ready to take the test' to 'I could not attend at the time set' along with all the usual personal issues.

Participation in the formative assessment is important to the feedback/learning cycle as it enables identification of difficult topic areas and as a consequence more focus can be given to those subject areas. This two-way feedback process can also be used by students to help them plan their final revision.

It is the intention of this case study to utilise technology to devise some formative assessments that will be more closely aligned with the final CBA. It is hoped that the use of Moodle will provide a virtual learning environment which will enable students to sit the assessments at a location and time that is more convenient to them. This flexibility may overcome some of the common problems (eg distance from university) and encourage more students to participate.

As the assessments will be made up of objective test questions including multiple choice, a further benefit expected to arise from the use of Moodle is that they will be marked instantly with immediate electronic feedback to the student.

Questionnaires will be used to gather student feedback relating to the modules already sat this year where Moodle was not used and also for the modules which will be assessed in June 2010 where Moodle will be used. This will enable a comparison to be made of the student experience and an appraisal of whether using Moodle has increased student participation.

The case study will also investigate whether embracing computer based assessment at the formative stage in a less formal environment impacts positively on the first time pass rates in the externally set summative assessment.

POT Moodle: Practice Oppposing Technology (P.O.T.) in the Moodle electronic submission pilot.

Rosemary Eaton and Mike Reddy

Newport Business School, University of Wales, Newport, Allt-yr-yn Campus, Allt-yr-yn Avenue, Newport, NP20 5DA. Email: Rosemary.Eaton@newport.ac.uk; Mike.Reddy@newport.ac.uk

The electronic submission pilot, currently under way using mLE Moodle, attempts to reduce or remove the need for paper based submissions. There are many logistic advantages to direct submission via a digital interface. However, this is a radical change in practice: verification and audit trails for paper-based submissions have traditionally gone through the administrators; reliance on a Web 2.0 application is novel (at best) for many staff and students, who may not be sufficiently IT literate; and electronic feedback almost requires electronic marking, which itself presents major changes in practice for most lecturers.

This paper/presentation discusses two widely different module requirements for submission and marking, and looks at how Moodle use as well as module support was adapted to provide the best experience for both staff and students. It will attempt to highlight where there may be advantages over the current paper based submission and also identify some ways to overcome some of the difficulties encountered.

Furthermore, experience with the pilot has suggested several areas of concern over what exactly is best practice, and how close the experience should be modelled/adapted to existing working practices. For example, the use of Tablet PCs and eBook readers for digital marking is compared with the more traditional use of word documents, shared and annotated by separate markers prior to moderation.

Evidence of the experience from both students and staff involved with the electronic submission pilot will be presented.

Consequences of these experiences lead the authors to suggest that for the majority of staff and students, a significant support and training regime may be required to achieve the positive aspects of an electronic submission/marking scheme.

You can lead a horse to water (or a student to on-line resources).

Tom Webster and Jill Baird

School of Health and Social Science, University of Wales, Newport, Lodge Road, Caerleon, South Wales, NP18 3QT. Email: jill.baird@newport.ac.uk

Teaching undergraduate students in the modern educational arena allows for greater innovation in course material delivery and additional methods of encouraging student engagement. However as the intake for an undergraduate course is diverse it inevitably includes people who are more and less willing to engage with these alternative methods of learning. This project explored the medium of on-line quizzes as a tool to encourage students' engagement and learning. In this project 3 on-line quizzes were provided for students to engage with after the relevant material had been presented in class. The quizzes where made available to all students to facilitate engagement and learning, regardless of whether they would eventually opt to become participants in the study. Overall uptake of the quizzes was relatively low at 17%. A paper based questionnaire was used to investigate the motivations and constraints that allowed for and limited participation in the on-line quizzes. In addition to this a comparison was made between engagement in quizzes, engagement for the module as measured by course attendance, and student learning as measured by overall academic performance for the module.

Research challenges for technology enhanced learning: emerging themes from the TLRP TEL research programme.

Richard Noss

London Knowledge Lab, Institute of Education, University of London, 23-29 Emerald Street, London WC1N 3QS. Email: r.noss@ioe.ac.uk

I will describe the work of an ambitious 4-year Technology Enhanced Learning (TEL) research programme in the UK (www.tlrp.org/tel) and present some interim results as well as emerging themes from the work. The programme is funded for four years jointly by two UK Research

Councils (the Engineering and Physical Sciences Research Council – which handles Computer Science research – and the Economic and Social Research Council – which includes Education). This program seeks genuine innovation in both the learning sciences and computer science, and to achieve interdisciplinary collaboration that tackles issues of research design and the transformation of practice.

To what extent are the needs of students with disabilities met in a University Library Service.

Jason Murphy and Martin Edwards

Newport School of Education, University of Wales, Newport, Lodge Road, Caerleon, South Wales, NP18 3QT. Email: jason.murphy@newport.ac.uk

Over the past fifteen years government legislation has had a major impact on the number of disabled students entering university. In 1995 the Disability Discrimination Act came into being and made it unlawful for a disabled person to be discriminated against in employment. May 2001 saw the introduction of SENDA (Special Education Needs Disability Act) this act had far greater implications towards higher education. It was an amendment to Part IV of the Disability Discrimination Act 1995 and defined discrimination as the failure to make reasonable adjustments or unsympathetic behaviour to a student with a disability. SENDA (2001) made it illegal for a disabled person to be discriminated against and created major obstacles for universities who had to make reasonable adjustments to their admission and enrolment processes, teaching, assessment and support services.

The HESA (Higher Education Statistics Agency) have published since 1999 a breakdown of the figures for disabled students in higher education studying either undergraduate or postgraduate degrees. In 1998 – 1999 the figures suggest that 3.8% (26,432 students) of the student population were disabled this figure had grown to 7% of the student population by the 2007 – 2008 academic year. Despite there being a growth in the number of disabled students entering higher education there is a lack of knowledge about the student's experience from this diverse population.

SYMPOSIUM - STUDENT DIVERSITY AND ENGAGEMENT

New horizons on the literacy landscape: developing student writing in Higher Education.

Nicola Woods and Rachel Stubley

Newport School of Education, University of Wales, Newport, Lodge Road, Caerleon, South Wales, NP18 3QT. Email: Nicola.woods@newport.ac.uk, rachel.stubley@newport.ac.uk

There is increasing concern that the levels of literacy achieved by graduate students has declined over recent years and the salient perception is one of "deteriorating standards" (Street 2004). As we plan and develop our learning and teaching strategies, respond to the demands of our stakeholders (especially employers) and, most importantly, ensure the best educational opportunities for our students, it is vital that we address the thorny issue of literacy.

Not only do we need to consider how best to develop current students' literacies for future life, we also need to contemplate which forms of literacy will be relevant and valuable for our future students. Demographic shifts, social inclusion policies, the international agenda – all these are factors leading towards an increasingly varied student population in Higher Education. How can we meet the needs of our increasingly diverse students and ensure that they are provided with the best opportunities to develop literacies relevant for work and lifelong learning?

Adopting an ethnographic approach, the research reported in this paper seeks to elicit expectations and interpretations that students (and tutors) have regarding the development of written literacies. The paper reports on two aspects of the ongoing research project: (i) an analysis of focus groups held with over fifty undergraduate students; (ii) excerpts from students' video diaries recorded whilst undertaking written assignments.

Qualitative analysis of this data provides insights on questions including: what is meant by a 'good' academic essay (and do students and tutors agree on the answer to this question)?; what are students' ambitions in constructing a piece of writing (and do these reflect the ambitions of tutors)?; what do students find difficult about writing and how do they develop their skills (which resources do they find useful and who do they turn to for support)?; and finally, do students feel that they are able to represent their own experiences and opinions in their writing - to use their own voice?

Discussion centres on academic writing as social practice (Lea & Street 1998). Noting that the multiple literacies that students bring with them to university are often negated in the HE classroom, we consider ways in which learning and teaching practices can draw upon students' own views and values. We conclude that utilising the experience and expertise of our diverse students will best facilitate routes to the development of relevant and valuable literacies for both current and future students.

Executive functioning skills and utilisation of support in Higher Education students.

Amanda Kirby, Lisa Edwards, Sarah Jackson and Debra McCarney.

Newport School of Education, University of Wales, Newport, Lodge Road, Caerleon, South Wales, NP18 3QT.

All students starting out at university face a huge adjustment both in living and academic working, and there are many essential skills needed in order to be an effective Higher Education student. If students have a problem with any of the skills that fall under the Executive Functioning (EF) umbrella, they are likely to struggle with university life. Executive functioning describes independent and purposeful behaviour and encompasses many cognitive processes such as organisation, time management, prioritisation problem solving, planning, monitoring, and focussing and maintaining attention. All of these are essential skills needed to be an effective student in higher education. Evidence of increased levels of EF difficulties has been shown in students with Dyslexia, Autism Spectrum Disorder, Attention deficit/hyperactivity disorder (ADHD) and Dyspraxia (also known as DCD), thus suggesting that there may be an increased need to offer EF skills support to these students. In the UK, 2.9% of undergraduates have been reported to have dyslexia or ASD (HESA stats, 2006). There are no UK statistics on numbers of students with DCD and ADHD, however it is estimated that ADHD symptoms affect 2% to 4% of the American college student population (DuPaul et al., 2001), with similar numbers existing for DCD.

Two hundred and eleven UK Higher Education students completed a questionnaire designed to examine executive functioning abilities and use of supportive strategies. One hundred and ten students identified themselves as having difficulties with organisation skills or were accessing student support services (the difficulties group), the remaining one hundred and one students did not have any difficulties or diagnoses of learning difficulties (the typically developing group). The difficulties group were noted to experience significantly more difficulties with study skills and executive functioning, compared to the typically developing group. This was evident in areas such as misreading assignment titles, prioritising work, organisation, goal setting and time management. The difficulties group were also noted to use less supportive aids than the typically developing group; 20% of the difficulties group 'often' or 'always' used past exam papers for revision, compared to 36.6% of the typically developing group and 16.4% of the difficulties group 'often' or 'always used a study partner, compared to 34.7% of the typically developing group. Similarly, 24.5% of the difficulties group 'never' used student services

Results have strong implications for Higher Education Institutions who may need to identify and address EF difficulties in their student populations in order to prevent risk of 'drop out' from courses or 'lower than expected performance' in students with EF difficulties. There also appears to be a clear need to review the format of support offered via student services as it appears that students with difficulties may not be utilising them to their advantage.

Problems students with learning disabilities experience in Higher Education: the study skills tutors perspective.

Jason Murphy

Newport School of Education, University of Wales, Newport, Lodge Road, Caerleon, South Wales, NP18 3QT. Email: jason.murphy@newport.ac.uk

Although more students are entering university with learning difficulties, their learning needs are not clearly understood. This study describes the findings and examines the issues arising from a small scale investigation into the problems encountered by disabled students through the eyes of their study skills tutors, and makes recommendations for policy and practice. The Methodology involved the use of a focus group with participants revealing their individual experience of supporting students with a learning disability and the problems they encounter on a day-to-day basis.

This study identifies from the focus group problems that students are experiencing in higher education and then provides examples of teaching strategies that create a positive learning experience for students with a learning disability. The implications for policy and practice are discussed and conclusions drawn including: the need for a central policy on inclusive curriculum which supports an inclusive learning environment for all students; policy and procedural change at an institutional level to ensure all courses have organisational strategies build in to support learning; staff training.

Wellbeing and engagement with Higher Education.

Kelly McCarthy

Centre for Community and Lifelong Learning, University of Wales, Newport, Lodge Road, Caerleon, South Wales, NP18 3QT. Email: Kelly.McCarthy@newport.ac.uk

Through investigative research, the notion of wellbeing and wellbeing indicators is explored in terms of how the notion itself can be interpreted, how it relates to engagement with higher education and, using wellbeing indicators as a tool, questions whether the unquantifiable can become quantifiable.

Wellbeing indicators are currently used in various different settings including mental health sectors and community development environments as a tool to map the wellbeing or quality of life of individuals. The 'soft outcomes', i.e. confidence, wider social networks, transferable skills, personal development, etc… of CCLL (Centre for Community and Lifelong Learning) students have traditionally been unquantifiable whilst simultaneously valid and valuable. The wellbeing research was born out of this problem and has explored whether wellbeing indicators could be utilised within CCLL and possibly across the wider institution. The tentative idea suggests that students could complete a set of indicators at the start of their engagement with higher education (HE) and then continue to complete them at intermittent points of study. In effect, this would map their subjective wellbeing against their higher education experience. The beauty of it would be that they would set their own baseline in terms of their own subjective wellbeing and any fluctuations would only be compared with existing and future wellbeing 'scores'.

Using a mixed methodology of quantitative and qualitative methods of data collection, the research has come to some conclusions on the value, practicality and usability of such a tool as wellbeing indicators in a higher education environment.

An overview of the research findings so far are presented in addition to some indications of where to go next and questions to stimulate debate.

SYMPOSIUM - SUSTAINABILITY AND GEOSCIENCE RESEARCH IN HIGHER EDUCATION

'Stop the bus, we want to get on!' Drivers of Education for Sustainable Development and Global Citizenship (ESDGC) in Welsh Higher Education.

Alison Glover

Centre for Excellence in Learning and Teaching, University of Wales, Newport, Lodge Road, Caerleon, South Wales, NP18 3QT. Email: Alison.glover@newport.ac.uk

The Talloires Declaration made by University Administrators in 1990 saw the real emergence of a raised and recognised profile of the importance of sustainability within the higher education arena. Prior to this the first mention of sustainability in higher education, in the international context, was highlighted by the United Nations in 1978, UNESCO – UNEP International Environmental Education Programme. Today documents and declarations continue to emerge in the endeavour to achieve effective sustainable development.

The Welsh Assembly Government published One Wales: One Planet in May 2009, outlining their commitment to embedding sustainable development as an organising principle across Wales within the vision of a 'transformed Wales'. For Our Future was also published in 2009 and identified aspirations for Welsh higher education. The role of Education for Sustainable Development and Global Citizenship (ESDGC) within higher education is fundamental in realising the visions proposed in these Assembly publications. Welsh higher education has placed increasing importance on ESDGC in recent years. A review of environmental management systems and an audit of ESDGC curriculum content complied with requirements of the Welsh Assembly Government and the Higher Education Funding Council for Wales. However, are there measurable indicators that reflect progress in effective sustainable development and global citizenship within an institution and across the Welsh higher education sector as a whole?

This paper focuses on the findings of recent research reviewing and analysing the relevance and validity of some existing measurable indicators for sustainability. Since 2005 the Green Gown Awards have recognised higher education's achievements in this area. The People and Planet Green League table was first published in 2007, with higher education institutions submitting information each year to be congratulated on their improvements and exposed for their inactions. Annually higher education institutions participate in environmental management schemes and citizenship awards.

This research endeavours to discover whether measurable progress in the higher education sector corresponds with the drive for a sustainable vision by the Welsh Assembly Government.

In the kitchen, but not in the classroom.

Tatiana Diniz

Centre for Excellence in Learning and Teaching, University of Wales, Newport, Lodge Road, Caerleon, South Wales, NP18 3QT. Email: tatiana.diniz@newport.ac.uk

The presentation will spot on some of the findings obtained by observing the delivery of Education for Sustainable Development and Global Citizenship (ESDGC) within four modules taught by CCLL (Centre for Community and Lifelong Learning, University of Wales, Newport). Following the WAG educational approach, CCLL is embedding ESDGC in all the disciplines offered in its centres. As part of a comparative study undertaken towards a PhD, I have observed lectures in different courses offered by CCLL during the Autumn Term in 2009 (Inequalities and Identities, Crime Fiction, Poetry and Contemporary Family). Methods also included questionnaires and interviews with students and tutors. Findings suggested that students perceive they are gaining knowledge about ESDGC, but this knowledge is not necessarily started up within the classroom or by the course's content. Apparently, informal approaches to ESDGC, from signs on the walls to self-organized practice of reusing and recycling amongst students are also giving relevant contribution. Discussions may point out to future possibilities of educational projects led by Higher Educational Institutions within community learning settings.

An holistic and multidisciplinary approach to volcanic risk assessment at Volcán de Colima, Mexico: A case study for modern management teaching.

Owen Landeg[1,2], Anthony J. Harris[1] and Mark Ware [2]

[1] Division of Sport and Science, Faculty of Health, Sport and Science, University of Glamorgan, UK.
[2] GIS Research Unit, Faculty of Advanced Technology, University of Glamorgan, UK.

This research explores the application of GIS models as a platform for assessing the risk posed by stratovolcanoes to modern civilisations. The completion of this research programme will further knowledge in the topical fields of natural hazards and crisis management, whilst demonstrating the far-reaching capabilities and benefits of a multidisciplinary approach to their mitigation.

On a regional scale, the resultant interactive GIS-based management tool will fully document the hazard posed by Volcán de Colima and serve as a vital resource that will benefit the Centre of Exchange and Research in Volcanology, University of Colima and the Colima Volcano Observatory, along with the wider scientific community. Furthermore, the knowledge gained through the successful completion of this research programme will demonstrate the potential hazard posed to those 390,000 people living within a 40Km radius of Volcán de Colima (González et al., 2002) and significantly aid the Civil Protection Agency charged with the implementation of mitigation techniques.

The impact of future volcanic unrest may be minimised, if not diminished, through effective, strategic assessment, planning and mitigation. The importance of detailed hazard assessments is best documented by Decker and Decker (2006), who state that in order to effectively reduce volcanic risk over the next century; the application of currently known methods must be undertaken in a more widespread manner. With recent signs of increasing explosive activity and a climactic, high-magnitude eruption predicted within the first quarter of this century (Luhr and Carmichael, 1980), the need for scientific exploration is imperative at Volcán de Colima.

This research programme, developed from previous research (Landeg, 2006), therefore challenges the present situation whereby less than ten per cent of the Earth's 1300 potentially active volcanoes have been adequately mapped to determine their likely hazard and addresses the critical need for scientific research at Volcán de Colima identified by Galindo and Domínguez (2002).

The incorporation of data concerning vulnerability parameters derived from census data and the results of a questionnaire exercise investigating the indigenous attitude and perception of risk provide a robust, holistic and contemporary methodology for volcanic risk assessment.

Using Volcán de Colima as a case study, my research-led teaching of final year geography and geology undergraduates at Glamorgan emphasises the importance of understanding the social matrix of a population as well as the spectrum of hazards posed by volcanic edifices. In order to fully understand the difficulties faced whilst managing a volcanic crisis, we have adapted a crisis simulation created by Harpp & Sweeney (2002).

The simulation requires students to work effectively within a group based upon the USGS Mobile Response Team and record and interpret incoming scientific data, to decide upon a suitable alert level and disseminate evacuation recommendations and scientific justification to a non-scientific audience, in this instance, the Governor of Colima. The undertaking of this simulation, coupled with the background of activity at Volcán de Colima provides the student with a novel teaching platform that has proved considerably successful and enhanced the student learning environment.

Climate change education: its importance post-Copenhagen and 'climategate'.

Simon K. Haslett

Centre for Excellence in Learning and Teaching, University of Wales, Newport, Lodge Road, Caerleon, South Wales, NP18 3QT, United Kingdom; Email: Simon.haslett@newport.ac.uk

The public perception of climate change has taken a battering over the last few months with the reported failure of the *Copenhagen Climate Summit* in December 2009 coinciding with the scientific scandal that has become 'climategate', and to top it all the United Kingdom has experienced its coldest winter for 30 years! Members of the public now often confront me with "surely global warming is a scientific myth"? Couple this with the growing 'green fatigue' that students display in learning about climate change, then it is clear that climate change education is facing unprecedented challenges at present, but at the same time, and for these reasons, has never been as important. Higher education should be taking a lead and it is significant that the publication of *Pedagogy of Climate Change* is imminent and that *C-Change* has been launched (a suite of open educational climate change and sustainability resources in the Geography, Earth and Environmental Sciences). These resources are an important development, but it is what lecturers and institutions do with them in their teaching and learning environments, and what students do with what they learn as a result that is the real climate change challenge.

Lessons learnt of post-tsunami reconstruction - experience of the Maldives.

Ali Rasheed

Auckland University of Technology, 55 Wellesley Street East 1010, Private Bag 92006, New Zealand; Email: arasheed@aut.ac.nz

Maldives and its Atolls are unique because of its geological and topographic aspects and their fragile and delicate environmental system. This can be seen, from the acceleration of coastal erosion that causes greater frequency of storms and flooding to these islands, and the threat of sea level rise, that threatens the existence of this archipelago of very small islands. While such changes may pose a threat to a small community of 300,000 people living in these islands, their more immediate impact can be seen on the right to adequate housing, in a country where land is very scarce and high population density is an issue in many islands. The post-Tsunami reconstruction process in Maldives has been a painful journey to the victims of 2004 boxing day tsunami. Decade after the Tsunami they have still been subjected to substandard housing and poor living conditions. Decisions to move them to other islands have caused problems of social integration. The lack of participation in the decision making process concerning relocation to the new settlements have proven to be unsuccessful in relation to the design of the new houses, and the infrastructure. Moreover, some engineering projects have been carried out without proper environmental assessment. The poster will show some of these scenes and challenges that small communities are faced.

SYMPOSIUM - CREATIVE ASSESSMENT, CURRICULUM AND PEDAGOGY

Towards a digital enlightenment: transformations of learning, thinking and creating in Higher Education.

David Longman

Newport School of Education, University of Wales, Newport, Lodge Road, Caerleon, South Wales, NP18 3QT. Email: david.longman@newport.ac.uk

In this paper I explore the complex challenges faced by HE in a reslutely digital culture. Two particular challenges will be the focus: (i) general: an exploration and evaluation of the discontinuity between the academic methods of HE and the culturally acquired assumptions and digital practices of undergraduates about knowledge making and taking; (ii) specific: the case of plagiarism and the practice of 'cut-and-paste' creativity as a particular example of a perceived threat to academic integrity in certain areas of academic culture.

Developing Enterprising Students

Richard Jeans and Emma Forouzan

Research and Enterprise Department, University of Wales, Newport, Allt-yr-yn Campus, Allt-yr-yn Avenue, Newport, NP20 5DA.

Entrepreneurial universities are considered to be vital to the UK's economy and society, developing enterprising graduates and staff and facilitating effective knowledge exchange between organisations. Reporting on the findings of a Learning and Teaching award, the presenters will discuss the characteristics of an entrepreneurial university, approaches to enterprise and entrepreneurship education and practices which that support the development of enterprising students.

Creative spaces.

Molly Owens

School of Art, Media and Design, University of Wales, Newport, Lodge Road, Caerleon, South Wales, NP18 3QT.

How does the environment in which we learn and teach influence our creative process?   How can we manipulate the space around us to enhance student productivity and the quality of student work?

These two questions form the basis of my research entitled 'Creative Spaces' that began in October 2009. As teachers, we are limited to the space we are given, but what can we do to manipulate that space and produce a successful learning experience?

During the course of two semesters, I undertake a series of exercises meant to determine how we can enhance the creative process without detracting from learning objectives and outcomes.   These exercises and experiments are conducted inside the classroom and out, to determine how space can be used to enhance student creativity and the student experience. Exercises, student participation and projects, field notes, and surveys will comprise the scope of this research. Joint projects within other disciplines also are undertaken as part of this research.

In addition, I interview a series of professionals who work in the creative industries, as well as those that work in traditionally 'non-creative' spaces (yet produce amazingly creative thinking processes). I see the potential for a link with industry in determining an environment suited to obtaining professional goals.

This research has already greatly assisted me in my own teaching practice. I believe this information will assist other in enhancing the student experience learning outcomes.

I will be creating original artwork (inspired by this study) to be exhibited in the Ffloc Gallery during the conference. This work is funded in part by a grant from the University of Wales, Newport (RSS Grant). The exhibition is being organised in conjunction with my colleague, Elizabeth Nelson. Our papers are linked, and Miss Nelson has submitted a proposal to present at the Nexus Conference as well.

Effectiveness of activities in science education for access to nursing students.

Craig Sims

Newport School of Education, University of Wales, Newport, Lodge Road, Caerleon, South Wales, NP18 3QT. Email: craig.sims@students.ac.uk

This project investigates the effectiveness of using a range of activities and teaching styles in the teaching of Science to Access to Nursing Students. The lessons utilise a range of teaching styles to allow a range or learning styles to be accommodated and also to induce cognitive dissonance through some activities to enhance learning outcomes.

Two groups of students were alternately delivered lessons in either an interactive or purely didactic manner. The responses of the students were assessed in three ways. Questionnaires utilising Likert scales were administered following each teaching session. Multiple choice tests were conducted as a summative assessment of each lesson. Interviews were used to assess both the outcomes and student responses to the two styles of lessons and gain feedback from teaching colleagues.

The results show that the interactive lessons significantly increased the scores of the students in a multiple choice test (P <0.0001) and the questionnaires showed a significantly higher overall regard for the Interactive lesson style (P <0.0001), conversely the when asked about the anxiety levels of the activities no difference was seen between the two lesson styles. The interviews supported the view that the students were more engaged and interested in the lesson. They also said they would prefer more lessons to be taught in this style

The result of the project is evidence that the use of a varied lesson with some activities designed to induce cognitive dissonance was able to significantly improve the learning outcomes of students and that the students were happy to comply. The evidence shows that they actually preferred the use of this lesson style. The down side of this style of teaching is that this type of lesson takes longer to prepare and organise as well as being potentially more expensive to run.

SYMPOSIUM - POSTGRADUATE AND ACADEMIC DEVELOPMENT

A tale of two Centres: comparing academic development in research-intensive and teaching-focused universities.

Cynthia Weston[1] and Simon K. Haslett[2]

[1]McGill University, Department of Educational and Counselling Psychology, Teaching and Learning Services. McLennan Library, 3459 McTavish Street, Montreal, Quebec H3A 1Y1, Canada. Email: Cynthia.weston@mcgill.ca

[2]Centre for Excellence in Learning and Teaching, University of Wales, Newport, Lodge Road, Caerleon, South Wales, NP18 3QT, United Kingdom. Email: Simon.haslett@newport.ac.uk

Within Higher Education there is a growing appreciation of the benefits of professional development for academics in teaching and learning, assessment methods, and curriculum development. Many institutions have established centres that have responsibility for delivering professional development events and courses for academics, and although the goal for each of these centres is similar, each faces an array of different challenges in engaging academics depending on the character of the institution. In this paper, two directors present their centres and review the challenges they face within their institutions. The two centres are compared and contrasted, as one, the Teaching and Learning Services, is located in a research-intensive Canadian university (McGill University), whilst the other, the Centre for Excellence in Learning and Teaching, is from a teaching-focused university in the UK (University of Wales, Newport). An international dimension is also noted, in that UK institutions have adopted a Professional Standards Framework, coordinated by the Higher Education Academy, whilst the Canadian sector lacks such an overarching framework.

It's not teaching – it's a PhD!

David Smith

Newport School of Art, Media and Design, University of Wales, Newport, Lodge Road, Caerleon, South Wales, NP18 3QT. Email:

The paper examines the pedagogical implications of some recent developments in the quality assurance of Research Degree supervision and training in the creative arts in the UK. PhD supervision is not usually thought of in this light, and yet may be seen as embodying an implicit pedagogy teetering uncertainly between watered-down social constructivism and a crudely osmotic version of "sitting with Nelly".

This is not an argument for taught doctorates, though these have their place. Rather, the paper questions the ability of the conventional mode of the Research Degree to deliver "original contributions to new knowledge", and argues that academics, and particularly those responsible for the management of postgraduate research degrees, must become more aware of current thinking in the pedagogy of creativity.

Some implications for the training of research degree supervisors and examiners will be presented and discussed.

Acknowledgements

The editors and conference organisers would like to thank the following for their assistance in producing this volume and organising the conference.

To the following organisations:

- The **Higher Education Academy Wales** for their association with the Conference.

- The **Higher Education Academy – Education for Sustainable Development Project** for supporting the Sustainability and Geoscience Research in Higher Education Symposium.

- The **Teaching and Learning Research Programme** for supporting the Technology Enhanced Learning Symposium.

- The **Atlantic Geoscience Society** for supporting the Sustainability and Geoscience Research in Higher Education Symposium.

To the following individuals:

- Symposium Chairs.
- All presenters and delegates at the Conference, and authors of written papers.
- CELT administrators – Vaida Andrijauskaite, Karen Jones, and Garry Jones.
- Newport Conference Office – Morna Manson, Emma Burnell and Alison Durston.
- Newport Associate Deans (learning and Teaching) and (Research and Enterprise).
- Marketing Department: Graham Harvey, Sian Crandon and Sarah Tilley.
- Other colleagues who have kindly helped.